TAKING ON TEHRAN

Strategies for Confronting the Islamic Republic

Taking on Tehran

Strategies for Confronting the Islamic Republic

Ilan Berman

LEXINGTON BOOKS

A division of
ROWMAN & LITTLEFIELD PUBLISHERS, INC.
Lanham • Boulder • New York • Toronto • Plymouth, UK

LEXINGTON BOOKS

A division of Rowman & Littlefield Publishers, Inc.
A wholly owned subsidary of The Rowman & Littlefield Publishing Group, Inc.
4501 Forbes Boulevard, Suite 200
Lanham, MD 20706

Estover Road
Plymouth PL6 7PY
United Kingdom

British Library Cataloguing in Publication Information Available

Library of Congress Cataloging-in-Publication Data

Taking on Tehran : strategies for confronting the Islamic republic / [edited by] Ilan
Berman.
    p. cm.
Includes bibliographical references.
ISBN-13: 978-0-7425-5806-9 (hardcover : alk. paper)
ISBN-10: 0-7425-5806-1 (hardcover : alk. paper)
ISBN-13: 978-0-7425-5807-6 (pbk. : alk. paper)
ISBN-10: 0-7425-5807-X (pbk. : alk. paper)
1. United States—Foreign relations—Iran. 2. Iran—Foreign relations—
United States. 3. United States—Foreign relations—2001- I. Berman, Ilan.
E183.8.I55T35 2007
327.7305509'0511—dc22   2007006842

Printed in the United States of America

The paper used in this publication meets the minimum requirements of American
National Standard for Information Sciences—Permanence of Paper for Printed Library
Materials, ANSI/NISO Z39.48–1992.

CONTENTS

FOREWORD

Thomas J. Ridge

Today, the United States faces no greater foreign threat than that from the Islamic Republic of Iran. And while the American public better understands this challenge with every day that passes, it is incumbent on our leaders in Washington to complement this awareness with action. Without a comprehensive policy that marshals all of our national assets and international leverage, Iran will march into the opening decades of the 21st century defiant, belligerent, virulently anti-American, and armed with a nuclear weapon.

Ironically, Iran was once one of America's greatest allies in the turbulent Middle East. Built around security and energy guarantees and a shared vision of modernity, the relationship between Washington and Tehran flourished for decades. In the process, the "Shah's Iran" became both a bulwark against Soviet expansion and a moderating influence on the radical fervor of its Arab neighbors.

This changed in 1979. The Islamic Revolution abruptly swept the Shah from power, installing in his stead a firebrand cleric, the Ayatollah Ruhollah Khomeini, as the Supreme Leader of a new, radical Islamic Republic. Ever since, the United States and Iran have been locked in a high-stakes struggle for power and influence, drifting further apart each time their interests collide.

Washington and Tehran's visions of the region could not be more different. The United States has earnestly tried to promote stability, encouraging Arab leaders to provide open political space to their disaffected publics, supporting reconciliation between Israel and the Palestinians, and moving assertively to neutralize regional radicals. Iran has done the opposite. No other nation on earth provides more financial, military and political support to Islamist terrorists. Today, the traditional balance of power in the Middle East is shifting toward Tehran, as Iran's geopolitical gains make the region less hospitable to the United States and American objectives. Additionally, the Iranian regime is on the verge of obtaining the technology necessary to build the most destructive weapon known to man.

In the past, when threats of this magnitude have emerged to challenge international peace and security, Europe and America could be counted on to work in tandem. Yet this unified West, which once faced down the demons of the 20th Century, is not what it once was and sadly not what it needs to be to confront this threat. Disagreement over tactics has stalled negotiations over the mildest, and potentially, least effective sanctions. Meanwhile, China and Russia, always mindful of their strong economic and energy ties to Iran, are predictably inclined to adopt a non-interference posture, dashing any hopes of concerted action at the UN Security Council in the process.

It is against this backdrop that this book has been written and among these pages that readers will find a call for action. It is important, for if the Iranian file does not sit atop the caseload of every relevant official in our national security apparatus, not enough is being done.

The challenge embodied by the radical, messianic President of Iran is unlike anything this country has yet confronted. In the 20th century, our enemies were evil, but they were rational; they cared little for human life, but a great deal about self preservation. These realities allowed for a window for compromise and negotiation to exist. Today, none does.

American policymakers must move quickly and decisively to confront the mounting menace posed by Iran and the pages that follow provide a number of suggestions on how to do so. They deserve the utmost attention of policymakers in Washington. For as we are beginning to realize all too clearly, the stakes in this struggle are far too high to allow Iran to impede a global desire for a more prosperous, more stable and less radical Middle East.

Introduction: Hard Choices

Ilan Berman

These days, ask almost any policymaker, expert or analyst what can be done about Iran, and you will get one of three answers. Some believe that the optimal way to deal with the Iranian regime's increasingly evident hegemonic ambitions in the Middle East is to reach some sort of negotiated accomodation.[1] Others say Iran's runaway nuclear ambitions constitute a *casus belli* that warrants the use of force.[2] Still others believe the ascendance of a nuclear or nuclear-ready Iran represents a benign, even beneficial, turn of events, and that no action at all is needed.[3]

None of these amount to a serious strategy. While it may reap short-term dividends for the United States, diplomatic engagement with the current regime in Tehran risks alienating Iran's young, pro-Western population—a vibrant constituency of some 50 million people aged 35 or younger that will ultimately determine the political disposition of that country. Military action is likewise deeply problematic, both because of the complexity of the strategic objective (neutralizing Iran's nuclear program) and because of the likely blowback such action will create from American allies and from Iranians themselves. Neither can Washington choose to simply do nothing, since our inaction will prompt a number of negative regional dynamics, ranging from a new arms race in the Middle East to the rise of a radical, anti-American Shi'a-dominated political order. Such is the sorry state of the policy debate over strategy toward the country that has emerged as the single greatest challenge to peace and stability in the greater Middle East, and to American interests there.

How did we get here? In truth, such policy confusion is not new. In many ways, it mirrors the political state of play regarding Iran that persisted throughout the mid- to late 1990s, when official Washington was divided between those who desired to modify the behavior of Iran's rulers, and those who sought a more fundamental transformation of the regime in Tehran. Back then, dreams of a reconciliation with the Islamic Republic led Washington to initiate a number of quiet overtures aimed at Tehran, only to be roundly rebuffed.[4] Iran's ayatollahs, it turned out, had little interest in normalizing relations with their longtime adversary, even if officials in Washington did.

Fast forward nearly a decade, and little has changed. Bogged down in Iraq and Afghanistan, the United States is undergoing a substantial attitude adjustment toward Iran. The Bush administration, which just one year ago proudly proclaimed its support for the desire for change visible among ordinary Iranians,[5] is now drifting toward accomodation with their regime. Meanwhile Iran's leaders, sensing America's weakness, have become increasingly bold, confrontational, and uncompromising in their worldview.

In other words, when it comes to Iran, America is suffering from an acute failure of imagination. And, without a serious strategy to confront Tehran, the potential consequences for the Middle East, and for the War on Terror, could be devastating. Already, Iran's advances have begun to alter the geopolitical balance of the Persian Gulf, much to the detriment of the United States and its Coalition allies. Iran's pervasive meddling in Iraq increasingly threatens to undermine U.S. efforts to create a stable, democratic order in the former Ba'athist state. Tehran's enduring support for international terrorism has increased the threat that radical groups such as Hezbollah, the Palestinian Islamic Jihad and al-Qaeda pose to the region, and to the West. And Iran's advances have already begun to reverberate throughout the region, threatening to dramatically reconfigure the politics of the greater Middle East—and to profoundly dampen future prospects for democracy there.

Now more than ever, policymakers in Washington need to think creatively about how to confront these trends. This book was written with that goal in mind, and the chapters that follow provide a number of political, economic and strategic building blocks of what would constitute a serious U.S. Iran strategy. They also offer a glimpse into the methods by which the United States can confront, contain and deter the Islamic Republic, and the impediments Washington will face in pursuing that goal.

The stakes are enormous. Without a serious plan to confront Iran, the United States in the near future will indeed be faced with just three choices: capitulation, confrontation or marginalization. For now, however, there is still time to prevent American interests in the Middle East from becoming the victim of Iran's successes. It is the sincere hope of the contributors to this volume that the U.S. government uses it wisely.

ENDNOTES

1. This is one of the core conclusions of the bipartisan Iraq Study Group chaired by former Secretary of State James A. Baker III and former Congressman Lee Hamilton. See *The Iraq Study Group Report* (New York: Vintage Books, 2006), 50-54.

2. Joshua Muravchik, "Bomb Iran," *Los Angeles Times*, November 19, 2006 , http://www.latimes.com/news/opinion/la-op-muravchik19nov19,0,1681154.story?coll=la-opinion-center.

3. French Foreign Minister Phillipe Douste-Blazy, for example, has gone so far as to say that Iran plays a "stabilizing role" in the Middle East. See Herb Keinon, "French FM: Iran a 'Stabilizing Force,'" *Jerusalem Post*, August 1, 2006, http://www.jpost.com/servlet/Satellite?cid=1153292045196&pagename=JPost%2FJPArticle%2FShowFull.

4. See Kenneth M. Pollack, *The Persian Puzzle: The Conflict Between Iran and America* (New York: Random House, 2004), 312-342.

5. President George W. Bush, State of the Union Address, Washington, DC, February 1, 2006.

Getting Smart on Iran

John C. Wobensmith

Today, precisely at the time when it needs such intelligence most, it has become abundantly clear that the United States knows precious little about the Islamic Republic of Iran. Indeed, years from now, America's current Iran quandary is likely to be seen as a case study of the necessity of dependable intelligence for conducting effective foreign policy.

This sorry state of affairs is certainly not new. It dates back to one of the greatest intelligence gaffes of modern times: the Carter administration's failure to accurately predict, and then to effectively respond to, the Islamic Revolution of 1979. Losing one of America's most important allies in the Middle East due to what was essentially a failure by the intelligence community to accurately comprehend the internal dynamics of a strategic ally was a foreboding hint of things to come.

The extent of America's intelligence gap with Iran became painfully evident in 2002, when a controversial Iranian opposition group disclosed that the Iranian nuclear program, bolstered by Russian and Chinese assistance, was in fact far more extensive and advanced than previously believed.[1] Subsequent investigations unearthed blueprints for nuclear weapons designs, traces of highly enriched uranium, and a plethora of previously clandestine documents and facilities, underscoring how little the United States and its allies actually knew about Iran's effort to acquire the "bomb"—sparking a frenzied effort to expand knowledge of Iranian capabilities.

More than four years later, the results have been decidedly mixed. Despite the narrow margin for error, the United States has thus far failed to convince the international community of the imminence of the Iranian threat. On the contrary, the U.S. intelligence community has produced a number of disparate and often contradictory conclusions about the nature and pace of the Iranian nuclear program, with deeply damaging results. Examples of this drift abound; back in 2003, the Defense Intelligence Agency and the U.S. government's Congressional Research Service estimated that, under the proper conditions, an Iranian "bomb" could be eight to ten years away.[2] Yet just two years later, in mid-2005, the U.S. intelligence community issued a new National Intelligence Estimate—subsequently leaked to the Washington Post—which assessed Iran to be at least a decade away from acquiring nuclear weapons.[3]

Today, these projections continued to widely diverge. In April of 2006, the Director of National Intelligence, John Negroponte, estimated that "it is still a number of years off before [Iran's leaders] are likely to have enough fissile material to assemble into or put into a nuclear weapon, perhaps into the next decade."[4] Yet just days later, Robert Joseph, the State Department's Undersecretary for Arms Control and International Security, claimed that Iran was "very close to that point of no return" in its nuclear development, and then-Defense Secretary Donald Rumsfeld publicly announced that he was "not confident" with Negroponte's assessment.[5] Others are even less sanguine; according to former Director of Central Intelligence R. James Woolsey, it is likely that Iran is just a year or two away from a weapons-usable capability at this stage in its nuclear development.[6]

Not only have these conflicting estimates sown discord at home, they have hampered consensus abroad. Needless to say, it is difficult to stress to a skeptical Chinese or Russian audience the immediacy of the Iranian threat when our own internal intelligence estimates conflict by as much as a decade. And, angered by America's perceived unilateralism in the run-up to the Iraq war, and by many of its policy choices thereafter, foreign audiences have become more skeptical than ever about such pronouncements from Washington.

Nor is Iran's nuclear program the only place where the intelligence community is falling short. In Iraq too, U.S. and allied intelligence services have been unable to measure the full extent of Iranian influence. To be sure, the U.S. had always expected such a state of affairs; the close ties, both historical and geographic, between the Islamic Republic and Iraq's large Shi'ite population made Iranian involvement all but inevitable. Yet the scope of Iranian penetration into its Arab neighbor has come as something of a surprise to the U.S.-led Coalition. Over the past three years, clear signs have emerged that Iran is engaged in a comprehensive political and strategic campaign on the territory of the former Ba'athist state. This effort includes support for and sponsorship of Iraqi Shi'a parties, such as the Supreme Council of the Islamic Revolution in Iraq (SCIRI), which is estimated to boast "at least 11,740" members on Iran's payroll within its armed militia wing, the Badr Corps.[7] Iranian agents are believed to have been transferring weapons and bomb-making technology to Iraqi insurgents and Shi'a militias in the country's south.[8] And leaked intelligence documents, off-the-record accounts, and regional experts all point to an Iranian regime that is "buying influence in the new Iraqi government, running intelligence-gathering networks and funneling money and guns to Shi'ite militant groups."[9]

In light of this conclusion, one might expect an aggressive response from the U.S. and its allies. Yet so far, there has been nothing—no direct military response, no trade sanctions, not even a Security Council resolution. The reason? At least as of this writing, a lack of the kind of incontrovertible evidence necessary to spur the skeptical international community into action. While officials in Washington, from President Bush on down, have charged that Iranian agents have been directly involved in attacks on Coalition troops,[10] hard evidence is difficult to come by. As then-Defense Secretary Donald Rumsfeld put it, "unless you physically see it coming in in a government-sponsored vehicle, or with government-sponsored troops, you can't know... it's very difficult to tie a threat precisely to the government of Iran."[11] The U.S. government cannot yet prove in any detail what everyone familiar with the Iraqi situation already knows; Iranian influence in the Iraqi south is pervasive, destabilizing and virulently anti-American.

As these two examples make abundantly clear, America's intelligence deficit on Iran is deep and long-running. The resulting failures have cost the United States dearly in the past, and will continue to do so as long as our understanding of Iran's domestic politics and foreign operations remains so woefully inadequate.

KNOWLEDGE GAPS

Reversing this dangerous trend requires the United States to "get smart" on Iran, and to do so very quickly. To do so, it needs to acquire information on five distinct fronts.

Political

Today, American policymakers have some insights into how policy decisions are made within the Iranian regime, and the roles that specific individuals play in the decisionmaking process. However, recent political changes have begun to alter the internal correlation of forces within the Islamic Republic, with potentially dramatic results for Iran's foreign and national security policy. One example is the Iranian presidency itself. Conventional wisdom has it that this is a largely ceremonial post, subservient to the country's clerical leadership in matters of strategic importance. This state of affairs certainly prevailed during the tenure of former president Mohammad Khatami (1997-2005). Khatami's terms in office were marked by dramatic challenges to his authority on the part of the country's Supreme Leader, the Ayatollah Ali Khamenei, and by a steady assault on the initiatives championed by the "reformist" cleric during his presidential campaign. By contrast, Iran's current president, Mahmoud Ahmadinejad, appears to wield far greater political control over regime strategy than his predecessor.[12] This difference is vital to understand; by gauging how much real power Ahmadinejad actually possesses, American policymakers can better determine whether his inflammatory anti-Semitic rhetoric and clearly apocalyptic religious leanings constitute mere bluster or are indicative of serious regime intent. Who is actually in charge in Tehran, in other words, matters a great deal, and should be an area of priority attention for the United States.

Equally important is insight into the internal dynamics among—and competition between—Iranian officials. In recent months, for example, Ahmadinejad's chief political rival, Expediency Council head (and former president) Ali Akbar Hashemi Rafsanjani, has gained substantial new political powers in a move seen by many as an effort by Iran's ayatollahs to constrain their maverick president.[13] Rafsanjani's newfound clout makes clear that the Islamic Republic is not a political monolith. To the contrary, Iranian politics are complex, convoluted and Byzantine in nature, and the United States needs a better understanding of the political competition taking place in Tehran—and of the existing fault lines between regime officials that potentially can be exploited by the West.

Most of all, however, decisionmakers in Washington need to know the weaknesses of their Iranian counterparts. During the Cold War, the Soviets elevated the collection of such information, known as kompromat, to an art form. Today, widespread corruption, social turmoil and cultural ferment have made the Islamic Republic a target-rich environment in this regard. By studying regime officials and learning their vices (including sexual habits, involvement in graft, drug use, and gambling, to name just a few), the U.S. intelligence community has the ability to identify leverage points that could be used against the Iranian leadership in times of crisis.

Military

Iran's strategic capabilities may now be the focus of intense international attention, but serious gaps in knowledge still remain. On the nuclear front, the Iranian regime has taken a lesson from the 1981 Israeli bombing of the Osirak nuclear reactor, and has hardened, separated and hidden its nuclear facilities. While some of these have since been uncovered, more information is needed about the true scope of Iran's nuclear endeavor. Simply put, in the event of military action, the United States cannot hope to neutralize Iran's atomic effort if it does not definitively know its size, sophistication and the locations of all critical facilities, including those responsible for command and control in times of crisis.

Similarly, better insights are needed into the human dimension of Iran's military might. Some soldiers matter more than others, and identifying key personnel—including political/military liaisons, special forces operatives, and civilian leaders—will help officials in Washington more effectively counter the regime's likely military strategy. It likewise is necessary for the U.S. to focus greater attention upon the Islamic Republic's military "brain trust:" the scientific and technical cadres that make Iran's military modernization and its work on high-tech weapons possible. Gaining access to the key scientists and engineers behind Iran's nuclear and ballistic missile programs will provide greater insights into the programs themselves.

Not all of Iran's military innovation is home-grown, however. The regime's nuclear program, for example, has benefited from extensive foreign assistance over the past decade-and-a-half.[14] Much of the critical intelligence regarding Iranian capabilities, therefore, resides in foreign hands, and contacts with scientists, technicians and specialists from abroad who have worked in Iran can yield fresh insights into the regime's capabilities and intentions.

Foreign assistance

Unlike the 1990s, when it was still by and large an international pariah, the Iranian regime today enjoys an extensive network of international partners. Some, like Russia, China and North Korea, have played important roles in furthering Iran's WMD efforts. Others, such as Venezuela and the countries of Central Asia and the Caucasus, have emerged as important economic allies of the Islamic Republic.

So far, these partnerships have proven durable, despite international concern over Iran's nuclear effort. But continued alignment is obviously contingent on the preservation of good diplomatic and strategic ties between those nations and the Islamic Republic. As a result, the United States must make it a priority to identify potential "wedge issues" between Iran and its strategic partners. Policymakers in Russia, for example, are deeply concerned about the potential for Islamist separatism in the "post-Soviet space." Evidence that Iran's ayatollahs are actively engaged in fomenting such instability, therefore, would serve to dramatically chill ties between Moscow and Tehran. Similarly, the strength of Iran's ties with another key international ally, China, depends greatly upon the Islamic Republic remaining a reliable energy supplier for the PRC. By learning more about the bilateral political ties between the Iranian regime and its foreign partners, the United States can identify wedge issues that would help to isolate Tehran internationally—and exploit them, if necessary.

Internal dynamics

Although contemporary intelligence collection tends to minimize this fact, not all countries are the same. An accurate understanding of local culture and psychology is essential to determining the likely reaction to planned action.

Domestic perceptions of Iran's nuclear program are a case in point. Although the Iranian leadership shares little in common with its restive population, the regime's concerted efforts to acquire a nuclear capability have resonated with ordinary Iranians. By all accounts, Iran's nuclear program is extremely popular on the Iranian "street," albeit for very different reasons than the ones motivating regime leaders to "go nuclear." As a result, external action that appears to be an effort to deprive the country of its right to nuclear energy is likely to prove seriously counterproductive, sparking a "rally around the flag" effect among ordinary Iranians and strengthening the true target of these measures—the Iranian regime—in the process. Simply put, accurate, timely knowledge about the psychology of the Iranian people is an important predictor of exactly what should be attempted as part of American strategy, and what policy options should be tabled.

Strength of the opposition

Irrespective of the strength of its intelligence, it is clear that the United States will not be able to shape Iranian behavior without assistance from the inside. This is why it is crucial to identify so-called friendly assets that are now "on the ground" inside the Islamic Republic. Such an effort needs to go beyond simply recruiting locals to serve as spies, to include greater knowledge about the various opposition groups now active against the regime in Tehran. Today, thanks to the Islamic Republic's aggressive persecution of regime opponents, the United States has far too little actionable information about the nature of viable opposition within Iran. Washington needs to know much more about who is good, who is bad, and who is irrelevant within the spectrum of current Iranian opposition. As part of this process, it will be necessary not only to identify regime opponents, but also to gauge their level of popularity among ordinary Iranians, as well as their degree of access to the inner workings of the regime—both crucial barometers for their future success.

AN INTELLIGENCE ACTION PLAN

In order to obtain this information, it will be necessary for the United States to take a number of steps.

The first is rebuilding its human intelligence, or HUMINT, capability within Iran. Networks of operatives, informants and other assets are the essential building blocks of the intelligence trade. Without them, policymakers are often left blind to the internal machinations of hostile regimes, and are surprised by otherwise foreseeable developments. HUMINT, however, is a fading art. Over the past three decades, the intelligence community has undergone a pronounced shift in emphasis, discounting the human element of intelligence gathering in favor of the more arms-length collection made possible by signals intelligence (SIGINT) technology. Yet, as the experience of the War on Terror thus far has eloquently shown, SIGINT, while a valuable tool in its own right, provides limited insights into the kind of cultural expertise, social savvy and political cunning necessary to operate in the Middle East. This state of affairs exists in spades for Iran, a country notorious for its political complexity and backroom politics. Yet, over the past several years, whatever meager HUMINT capabilities the United States possessed "on the ground" within the Islamic Republic have been identified, wrapped up and eliminated.[15]

Now more than ever, the United States desperately needs to rectify this dangerous deficiency. Part of rebuilding this HUMINT capacity involves training domestic assets and regional agents to conduct work inside Iran's borders—an area where America has lacked any significant intelligence presence since the late 1970s. A less obvious but equally important avenue is the encouragement of Western businessmen, scholars, doctors and academics with contacts in Iran, particularly those in Europe. All of the information to be garnered in this matter, regardless of its immediate relevance, is a valuable asset toward building a more comprehensive understanding of the Iranian regime.

American officials should make no mistake, however; such an effort will not succeed overnight. It will take a great deal of time and effort to reconstitute the meager capabilities that the U.S. intelligence community had on the ground at the time of the Islamic Revolution, and longer still to build networks robust enough to have truly predictive capabilities about the notoriously complex politics of the Islamic Republic.

The second area of focus for the American intelligence community needs to be linguistics. It is a poorly held secret in Washington that the U.S. government suffers from a shocking deficit of Farsi speakers and Iranian/Persian experts. This shortfall has serious consequences for our intelligence collection activities *vis-à-vis* Iran, hampering our ability to translate Iranian websites, newspapers, and communications, including those by dissident groups and opponents of the regime. Such capabilities are of historic and fundamental importance to any intelligence operation, and our current predicament speaks to both a lack of funding and an absence of political will within the intelligence community.

This problem is acute, and it is growing. Since much of the intelligence work to be done with regard to Iran will rest heavily upon American HUMINT capabilities, the United States should expect even greater strain to be placed on the limited number of Farsi linguists currently at the government's disposal. Expanding this cultural and linguistic base, therefore, should be a top priority, with monetary and social incentives offered to new recruits proficient in the culture/language set necessary for robust data collection regarding Iran.

A third priority for the United States should be the expansion of intelligence contacts with allied and friendly nations on the subject of Iran. If the United States suffers from an acute intelligence deficiency with regard to Iran, other countries do not. France, Germany, Italy, Great Britain, and Japan are just a few of the friendly nations that enjoy robust trade relations with Iran—and corresponding insights into Iranian economics, politics and society. Other nations, including Israel, Saudi Arabia and Turkey, historically have had adversarial relations with the Iranian regime, and the depths of their intelligence networks there reflect this fact. The United States needs to better leverage these latent assets. Through the establishment of technical collection bases in surrounding countries, the cooperative training of intelligence officers, and closer political collaboration, Washington can quickly and efficiently begin to make up its intelligence deficit on Iran.

Such cooperation is bound to come with political costs. Policymakers can and should expect *quid pro quos* for intelligence on Iran from friendly nations—ranging from the benign (satellite imagery and political support) to the problematic, including the forfeiture of assets elsewhere. Obviously, each such demand will need to be judged on a case-by-case basis, and the costs may well outweigh the benefits. Given the importance of the target nation, however, Washington would do well not to balk outright at such horse trading.

Finally, and most importantly, the American political leadership needs to clearly and unambiguously designate Iran as a top intelligence priority. The President must emphasize to the entire U.S. intelligence apparatus that the Iranian issue is henceforth its central task. Such a focus will require steady oversight, and the President and his top aides must be prepared to demand regular updates and recommendations by each department and agency involved in gathering intelligence on Iran. It will also require a reconfiguration of how such intelligence gathering is done. The current method, where material from a dozen or so agencies is filtered by the Director of National Intelligence into a unitary intelligence assessment, hampers the ability of the President to take into account differing viewpoints and creative or "out-of-the-box" suggestions. Indeed, the current process, focused as it is upon generating consensus within the intelligence community, tends to produce estimates that are based on the lowest common denominator. In the process, dynamic opinions and perspectives at odds with the *status quo* fall by the wayside, preemptively limiting the President's potential options. Today, by contrast, such opinions should be encouraged, and mechanisms that facilitate them should be fostered. Here, the White House can and should take a page from the Cold War playbook, establishing a "Team B" on Iran analogous to the group of foreign policy experts that produced parallel intelligence estimates on Soviet capabilities in the 1970s.

Clearly, there is no such thing as a quick fix to Washington's current intelligence deficit concerning Iran. Our lack of knowledge regarding the capabilities and intentions of the Iranian leadership is as old as it is glaring. And, at least for now, it shows no signs of abating. However, with greater funding, better oversight and—above all—the necessary political will, the United States can reverse its decades-long intelligence failure with regard to the Iranian regime. With the prospect of a nuclear Iran—and, potentially, of another war in the Middle East—hanging in the balance, there can be no task more crucial.

Endnotes

1. Robert G. Joseph, Statement Before the House of Representatives Committee on International Relations, March 8, 2006, http://www.internationalrelations.house.gov/archives/109/jos030806.pdf.

2. Kenneth Katzman, *Iran: Arms and Weapons of Mass Destruction Suppliers* (Washington: Congressional Research Service, January 3, 2003), http://www.fas.org/sgp/crs/nuke/RL30551.pdf.

3. Dafna Linzer, "Iran Is Judged 10 Years From Nuclear Bomb," *Washington Post*, August 2, 2005, A01.

4. John Negroponte, Speech before the National Press Club, Washington, DC, April 20, 2006, http://www.dni.gov/speeches/printer_friendly/20060420_speech_print.htm.

5. Phillip Kurata, "Iran Approaches Point of No-Return on Acquiring a Nuclear Program," U.S. Department of State *Washington File*, April 21, 2006, http://usinfo.state.gov/usinfo/Archive/2006/Apr/21-842193.html; Interview with Donald Rumsfeld, *The Laura Ingraham Show*, April 18, 2006, http://www.defenselink.mil/transcripts/2006/tr20060418-12862.html.

6. R. James Woolsey, Remarks at the American Foreign Policy Council Conference on "Understanding the Iranian Threat," Washington, DC, November 15, 2006, http://www.afpc.org/IFI/Woolsey.wmv.

7. Michael Ware, "Inside Iran's Secret War for Iraq," *Time*, August 15, 2005, http://www.time.com/time/magazine/article/0,9171,1093747,00.html.

8. "Blair Accuses Iran of Arms Supply." BBC (London), July 18, 2006, http://news.bbc.co.uk/2/hi/uk_news/politics/5190098.stm.

9. Ware, "Inside Iran's Secret War for Iraq."

10. Bill Brubaker, "Top U.S. Military Official: No Evidence of Iran Involvement in Iraq," *Washington Post*, March 14, 2006, http://www.washingtonpost.com/wp-dyn/content/article/2006/03/14/AR2006031401083.html.

11. Ibid.

12. See, for example, Ilan Berman, "Understanding Ahmadinejad," American Foreign Policy Council *Iran Strategy Brief* no. 1, June 2006, http://www.afpc.org/IFI/UnderstandingAhmadinejad.pdf.

13. See, for example, Ayelet Savyon, "The 'Second Islamic Revolution' in Iran: Power Struggle at the Top," Middle East Media Research Institute *Inquiry and Analysis* no. 253, November 15, 2005, http://memri.org/bin/articles.cgi?Page=archives&Area=ia&ID=IA25305.

[14] See, for example, Jack Boureston and Charles D. Ferguson, "Schooling Iran's Atom Squad," *Bulletin of the Atomic Scientists* 60, no. 3 (2004), 31-35.

[15] Author's interview with former U.S. special forces commando, Washington, DC, July 2006.

THE DANGERS OF DETERRENCE

James S. Robbins

While there is still hope that Iran will not develop nuclear weapons, it is becoming more likely that a nuclear-armed Iran will become a reality in the near future. Therefore, it is useful to begin looking at strategic models for managing the threat of nuclear weapons if Iran actually develops them, and to consider exactly what risks the civilized world would be facing.

There is a strong body of opinion that nuclear weapons contribute to international stability through deterrence. The consequences of nuclear war, the argument goes, are so grave that the mere threat of nuclear conflict is enough to discourage national decision-makers from seeking to resolve differences through the use of force. The U.S.-Soviet nuclear balance was the paradigmatic case in this regard. Since the end of the Cold War, this model has been applied to other circumstances, such as the strategic balance between India and Pakistan.[1] With respect to Iran, the analogy holds that a nuclear power equal in size and opposed to the Israeli nuclear arsenal will add to the overall stability of the region. Alternatively, Iranian nuclear force will be more than matched by that of the United States, which presumably would be used to respond to any use of nuclear weapons on the part of the Iranians. The end result would be either no significant change in the region, or a beneficial balance of tension.[2] This complacent "Cold War redux" point of view has been summarized as follows:

> Could the United States live with a nuclear-armed Iran? Due to U.S.
> strategic predominance, many experts believe the Iranian regime

would be unlikely to use its nuclear capability overtly unless it faced what it perceived to be an imminent and overwhelming threat. An Iran emboldened by nuclear weapons might become more assertive in the region, but superior U.S. conventional capabilities and strengthened regional partnerships would probably deter Iran from significant mischief, such as closing the Strait of Hormuz or attacking U.S. forces directly. The United States has options short of war that it could employ to deter a nuclear armed Iran and dissuade further proliferation. These include reassuring allies and friends in the region, strengthening active and passive defenses, improving preemption and rapid response capabilities, and reinforcing nonproliferation incentives and counterproliferation activities.[3]

Obviously, this argument places great faith in all parties accepting stability as a norm, as well as in the efficacy of diplomacy. Yet those who argue that the Iranian nuclear arsenal would be of little practical value must first address the simple fact that Iran is actively seeking such a capability. Presumably, the Iranian regime does not assume a nuclear arsenal would have little value, or it would not be devoting a substantial level of resources and trading a great deal of political capital in the pursuit of it.[4] Furthermore, nuclear deterrence reaches well beyond the basic assumption that countries will not employ nuclear weapons because of fear of a counterstrike, and several critical aspects of the traditional nuclear deterrence paradigm are not present with regard to Iran. Moreover, when one examines conflict beyond the high end of the spectrum, one discovers that nuclear deterrence, even when effective, can foment conflict at other levels, and can in fact be a destabilizing force.

REQUIREMENTS FOR DETERRENCE

The classic Cold War-era nuclear deterrence model posited a number of requirements beyond two countries possessing nuclear weapons.[5] While the lists vary from analysis to analysis, most include the following:

1. Both or all sides in the nuclear equation must be "rational actors." That is, they must be able to understand the threat posed by nuclear weapons, to value the same things (especially the preservation of life), and be able to see the disutility of nuclear conflict;

2. Both or all sides must possess a second strike capability, i.e., be able to absorb an enemy first strike and deliver a devastating counterattack;

3. All sides must have full knowledge of the size, composition and capabilities of enemy nuclear forces;

4. All sides must have clear, open and permanent means of communication, especially in times of crisis;

5. All sides must accept the deterrence paradigm, as well as the right of the other to exist as a sovereign state.

Each of these components is worth examining in turn.

Rationality

The "rational actor" assumption is critical to deterrence modeling. All sides must have confidence that adversary decision-makers are reasonable people, motivated by the same types of concerns and desiring to preserve peace and human life. Essentially, rational actors seek to maximize chances for survival. Regimes that have shown a propensity for random or unpredictable behavior do not fit the model well; in effect, they may not be able to be deterred because they may not fully understand the threat they face, or—worse yet—may not care about the consequences.

In the case of Iran, the term "rational" may be something of a misnomer. Rationality connotes an understanding of the relationship between means and ends, as well as knowledge of actions and consequences. With respect to deterrence, the assumption is that a rational person would not risk certain destruction in pursuit of national security objectives because the outcome would be contradictory – not security, but annihilation. However, it is possible both to be rational and to hold an entirely separate set of premises about the nature of that reality and the consequences of death. In other words, one may believe that there are greater interests than preserving life. The phenomenon of suicide terrorism is a case in point; a suicide bomber cannot benefit from the act of violence he or she perpetrates, at least not here on Earth. Yet some have decided that death is preferable to life under some form of oppression. Others see it as a way of achieving fame and veneration that they could gain any other way. Still others seek a reward in a presumed afterlife, an eternity in paradise in exchange for a moment of earthly brutality.

Whether the notion of suicide in pursuit of policy goals can be elevated to a national level remains to be seen. However, there is reason to believe that key members of the Iranian leadership are sympathetic to the *mahdaviat*, i.e., the belief in and efforts to prepare for the return of the so-called Hidden Imam, believed by many to be the Islamic messiah, or Mahdi.[6] Iranian President Mahmoud Ahmadinejad himself has stated that the Iranian Revolution's "main mission is to pave the way for the reappearance of the 12th Imam, the Mahdi."[7] Those beholden to this belief, moreover, foresee a time of chaos and violence, an apocalypse, which will serve as the catalyst for the Mahdi's return. While some debate whether or not human action can accelerate this event, the idea that this belief is prevalent in the Iranian leadership should give policymakers pause. A rational actor under the influence of *mahdaviatist* thought might well see nuclear conflict as an acceptable, even beneficial, option if it would hasten the timeline for human salvation. This is not a solid foundation for a nuclear deterrence framework.

Second-strike capability

Second-strike capability is the lynchpin of the doctrine of Mutual Assured Destruction (MAD). It is what makes destruction "assured," because no side can completely disarm the other by a sudden surprise attack. (It is "mutual" when both sides possess this capability, which is essential to the stability model.) Developing and deploying a credible second-strike capability requires years of work on weapons systems, strategies, training, and other aspects of the nuclear apparatus. In the case of the Middle East, this would require that any parties to the deterrence model undertake a massive arms buildup simply in order to acquire the capability to deter nuclear war.[8] This arms race, in turn, would likely spur proliferation to other countries in the region, which would multiply uncertainties. In addition, no country that accepts the MAD framework could deploy ballistic missile defenses, because the greatest level of stability is achieved when all countries are defenseless, making the enemy's second-strike capability more credible. This was the strategic logic that resulted in the 1972 Anti-Ballistic Missile (ABM) Treaty.[9] It is doubtful, however, that the belief in the stabilizing effects of defenselessness would quickly be embraced in such a volatile region.

Transparency

Transparency is necessary for effective nuclear deterrence. Each side must have as much information as possible about the enemy's nuclear capabilities in order to accurately understand the risks of taking action. Without this precise knowledge, the enemy's deterrent may lack credibility, which is itself a destabilizing factor. All sides must be confident that their arsenal would be able to survive an enemy strike, and at the same time, would not be able to totally destroy the enemy force if used offensively. In order to have this level of assurance, treaties or other forms of agreement that limit the number and type of forces each side may field need to be concluded. Moreover, inspection and verification regimes need to be put into place in order for each side to feel confident that the agreed-upon limits are being observed. It is highly unlikely that this type of complex structure could ever be put in place in the case of Iran; constructing a framework for transparency will be particularly difficult between countries that do not have diplomatic relations. And even during the Cold War, verification regimes had proved to be controversial and difficult to enforce. These problems would be magnified significantly in the Middle East.

Communications

In order for deterrence to be effective, all sides must be able to communicate clearly, openly and without interruption, especially during times of crisis. This is critical to building the kind of rapport that can minimize the risks of misunderstanding and avoid accidental war. During the Cold War, the most notable manifestation of this requirement was the "hot line" set up between the White House and the Kremlin in the wake of the Cuban Missile Crisis.[10] Similar communications mechanisms and protocols would have to be established in the Middle East, a project which would run afoul of the same issues and limitations as the transparency structure.

Acceptance of the status quo

Above all, the nuclear deterrence paradigm is rooted in the acceptance of the existence of one's adversary. It is a status quo orientation that does not seek revisionist changes to the system, at least not through the use of nuclear forces. The model also recognizes that promoting change by other means could result in destabilizing forces at the nuclear level, possibly leading to nuclear war. Yet, there is no reason to believe that Iran accepts the existence of Israel or respects that of the United States or other countries. Iran is an explicitly revolutionary state that openly preaches policies of radical change. A nuclear-armed Iran would not forego this long-standing revisionist posture, especially since it would be better able to pursue its objectives of regional change.

Bipolarity

Even if the abovementioned conditions could be met in the Iranian case, the classic nuclear deterrence model assumes a bipolar international (or in this case, regional) system. During the Cold War, this was a reasonable—if not completely accurate—assumption. Certainly, the preponderance of power rested with the U.S. and the Soviet Union; most models therefore ignored the French, British and Chinese nuclear arsenals. The reason for this neglect was clear: lesser forces tended to complicate the models, while bipolarity made abstract game theory more comprehensible and applicable.

However, the strategic situation in the post Cold War world is more complicated. The nuclear equation in the Middle East would clearly not be limited to Iran and Israel. The United States is a major potential participant in any nuclear crisis in the region, and other third parties may become involved as a nuclear scenario—whether Iranian-Israeli or other—begins to unfold. Russia, for example, might have an interest in seeking to balance U.S. forces in order to prevent the United States from intervening. China, concerned about access to energy, could also seek to bring nuclear pressure to bear. It is reasonable to suspect that Pakistan, India, North Korea, or the European nuclear states could also become involved if the crisis escalates. None of these countries needs actually to use their weapons to affect the nuclear balance. They only have to show a credible propensity to do so.

By the same token, the development of nuclear weapons in Iran could reasonably be expected to spur similar research and development efforts in neighboring states, particularly Saudi Arabia. It is hardly a coincidence that in November 2006, in the midst of growing international concern over Iran's nuclear programs, six Arab states announced that they themselves would be pursuing nuclear research programs.[11]

In short, it would be a serious error on the part of strategic planners to reduce the nuclear equation in the Middle East to a more easily comprehensible bipolar system, or to assume that the dynamics of the U.S.-Soviet rivalry are universally applicable to other countries and circumstances.

Focusing on deterrence suffers from another deficiency as well. It discounts the idea that Iran actually might be seeking a nuclear arsenal that would enable it to fight and win a nuclear war, particularly against Israel. If Tehran believed that it had a credible first strike capability against Jerusalem, i.e., that it could annihilate Israel's nuclear capabilities in one massive attack, the necessary logic of nuclear strategy would argue for launching what is known as a "bolt from the blue" surprise attack.

Here, skeptics might cite the existence of the U.S. nuclear umbrella, and the probability that Washington would retaliate against any such Iranian aggression. But this is a questionable rationale on which to base a deterrence model. It is possible that the United States might choose not to respond, if presented with a *fait accompli*. Nothing the United States could do would bring back what the Iranians had already destroyed. Moreover, going to war would not be risk-free. American decision-makers would have to weigh the mixed benefits of a nuclear strike against Tehran, potentially involving millions of civilian casualties, against the risk of an Iranian retaliatory nuclear attack on a major American population center. The question at that point would be: "is it worth trading New York for Tehran, in order to have justice for Jerusalem?" Would the United States place millions of American lives in jeopardy for the sake of its defeated ally?[12] The answer would probably be yes, but there would be strong voices in opposition. Furthermore, the very fact that American policymakers would have to take such questions into account is an example of deterrence in action.

DETERRENCE ACROSS THE CONFLICT SPECTRUM

Discussions of Iran's nuclear capability tend to focus on its effects at the high end of the conflict spectrum, i.e., the possibility of nuclear war and the prospects for deterring a nuclear exchange. However, nuclear deterrence has an impact at all levels of conflict: nuclear, conventional, and unconventional. Whether or not Iran can successfully be deterred from employing nuclear weapons in warfare, an Iranian nuclear force-in-being would have critical implications for international security, particularly in the Middle East region.

Deterrence at the nuclear level precludes one type of conflict, but in the process makes other, lesser forms more likely. Deterrence during the Cold War may be credited with preventing a global thermonuclear conflagration, but the period was not particularly peaceful. The conflicts in Vietnam and Afghanistan, Soviet interventions in Hungary and Czechoslovakia, the U.S. invasion of a Soviet client state in Grenada, numerous proxy wars and guerilla struggles, and the Soviet-sponsored international terror network, all attest to the lower-level violence that can proliferate under the nuclear umbrella.[13]

Both U.S. and Soviet decision-makers also sought to avoid escalation of local conflicts.[14] The war in Vietnam was the classic case; the United States, more powerful than North Vietnam and potentially able to defeat the communist client state militarily without resorting to nuclear weapons, chose to limit the manner in which the war was conducted out of concerns of escalation that could potentially involve the People's Republic of China and the Soviet Union, perhaps leading to a nuclear exchange. Washington did not seek decisively to defeat Hanoi because of the danger that such an effort might lead to a general war in Southeast Asia, or maybe even in Europe, in the latter case with probable nuclear consequences. Ultimately, the United States was prepared to accept defeat in Vietnam rather than risk escalation.[15] The willingness to suffer local defeats rather than risk the consequences of nuclear conflict is a powerful dynamic that disproportionately favors weaker and more erratic nuclear powers.

Thus, despite global American dominance in nuclear and conventional forces, the United States can be defeated when faced with a determined enemy with the ability to inflict violence at levels the U.S. finds unacceptable or disproportionate to its desired objectives. This underscores one reason why Iran may find nuclear weapons valuable: to enable conflict at lower levels of the conflict spectrum by engaging the fear of escalation. Because all actors possessing nuclear weapons may consider themselves safe from escalation to total war, they can fight at lower levels with relative impunity. Furthermore, the United States would have fewer options for pursuing a policy of regime change in Iran, since it would be unwise to place the current Iranian leadership in a situation where they were on the brink of downfall and had nothing to lose by launching a nuclear strike (see the scenario noted below), or one in which the regime lost control of its nuclear warheads in the ensuing chaos.

Use of force at the conventional level

Currently, the United States is the dominant conventional military force in the world. U.S. defense spending is two-thirds the aggregate defense budgets of the rest of the world combined, and is around 80 times greater than that of Iran.[16] The United States could reasonably be expected to prevail in a purely conventional struggle with almost any country. Furthermore, it is likely that any state defeated militarily by the United States would be encouraged to undertake a political reformation; in other words, experience a regime change. However, it is unlikely that the

---

U.S. would pursue such a conflict against a country with a nuclear capability. One wonders whether the United States would have been as able or willing to push to Baghdad in 2003 had Saddam Hussein's regime possessed nuclear weapons. The North Korean example is also salient here. Few now would suggest military intervention against Kim Jong-il's Stalinist state, largely because of the unpredictable consequences should North Korea use its presumed nuclear arsenal. What this illustrates is that possessing a nuclear capability can deter countries at the conventional as well as the nuclear level.

Yet such deterrence is not always equally balanced. A more erratic nuclear state seeking small-scale gains using conventional force may not face retaliation from the U.S. if the apparent risk is not perceived to be worth the potential gain. Thus, at the conventional level, the use of force would become more attractive to Iran, and simultaneously less so for the U.S. A nuclear-armed Iran might initially undertake minor conventional operations—such as seizing oil platforms in disputed waters or pressing claims against the Shatt al-Arab waterway by occupying small parcels of territory—as a way of testing American or regional resolve. Today, this type of overt Iranian conventional military action would be a *casus belli*, a provocation to which the United States could respond with massive and justifiable force. But if Iran were a nuclear power, U.S. decision-makers would have to think much more carefully about how to take action, and of what type. A military response would need to be limited, in order to prevent escalation. And whether or not they believed that Iran would use nuclear weapons in response to conventional military moves by the U.S. and its allies, Coalition planners would at least have to take the possibility into account. Furthermore, they would have to consider the possible responses of other nuclear-capable states that have interests in the region, as would the Iranians. It doubtless would be a more complex and dangerous decision matrix than any faced by policymakers during the days of Cold War bipolarity.

A number of hypothetical cases hammer home this point.[17] One is a scenario very familiar to U.S. war planners; the Iranian regime closing the Strait of Hormuz and subjecting the world to energy blackmail through an "access denial" strategy. Currently, the Coalition would respond by sending a flotilla to force an entry, probably accompanied by a punitive air campaign against high-value military, political or economic targets in Iran. At present, the Iranian regime would have no effective response. Yet a nuclear-armed Iran with medium-range missiles or other delivery systems would vastly complicate war planning. Carrier battle groups would have to be kept far out at sea. The intensity of the punitive air campaign would have to be weighed against the possibility that Tehran might seek to attack American domestic targets, perhaps with nuclear weapons. And policymakers would have to question the extent the United States would be able to rely on its Coalition partners in Europe if those countries were within range of nuclear-tipped Iranian missiles.

In another scenario, Iran launches a ground invasion through southern Iraq, into Kuwait, driving on Saudi Arabia. By doing so, Iran could seize control of four of the top five oil reserves in the world. Having taken the oil fields, Iran makes no further demands, and keeps the oil flowing. How would the international community respond, knowing that Iran would have recourse to nuclear weapons if military countermeasures were used? Would military action be taken at the risk of shutting off most Middle Eastern energy exports? Or would the international community conclude that the destabilizing risks of further conflict, made more so by the Iranian nuclear arsenal, were outweighed by the collective desire to maintain the uninterrupted flow of oil?

In a third scenario, the long-awaited democratic revolution begins to develop in Iran. Massive crowds turn out in the streets demonstrating against the increasingly harsh laws imposed by the radical government in Tehran. Students, liberals, labor groups, and even some army and police units begin to coalesce into a true revolutionary force. In response, the regime sends in its shock troops, the Pasdaran, to put an end to the unrest. In a Tiananmen Square-style crackdown, tanks roll in to crush (literally) the revolutionaries, who plead for Coalition intervention. In a non-nuclear environment, the U.S. could give the uprising enough air support and other assistance to at least stave off catastrophe, and maybe even to tip the balance in favor of the Iranian people—and do so with the approval of the majority of the international community. If the regime had nuclear weapons, on the other hand, it is doubtful that the U.S. would risk intervention. Moreover, the international community might actually oppose support for the Iranian democracy movement, fearful that Iran's leaders would launch a last-minute Armageddon-style conflict if they faced overthrow and sensed they had nothing to lose.

Nuclear weapons and terrorism

It will be at the unconventional warfare level, however, where the destabilizing effects of nuclear deterrence will be felt most. During the Cold War, the Soviet Union backed communist guerilla movements to further Moscow's strategic aims by means short of conventional conflict.[18]

The United States responded, also within a limited war framework, with the Reagan Doctrine of support for anti-communist insurgencies. Such proxy wars are attractive to nuclear powers because they have little chance of escalating, they do not involve potentially costly large-scale troop deployments, and they allow the maintenance of plausible deniability.

Iran has long been a state sponsor of proxy terrorist groups, the most noted of which is Lebanon's Hezbollah.[19] The United States tangled with the Iranian cat's-paw during the 1982-84 intervention in Lebanon; Hezbollah is generally believed to have been the force behind the 1983 bombings of the Marine barracks and U.S. embassy in Beirut, as well as the abduction and murder of CIA Station Chief William Buckley and other Americans. (Iran and Hezbollah have denied many of these charges, consistent with the plausible deniability rationale.) Hezbollah remains one of Iran's most effective tools for influencing events in the region, and the group is known to possess global reach. Iran's propensity to utilize terrorists and other front groups to pursue its interests is unlikely to diminish with the advent of an Iranian bomb, and in fact should increase as the regime feels increasingly safe from significant retaliation. Therefore, one could expect a rise in terror attacks and insurgent activity in areas where Iranian interests were in play.

Beyond the energizing effect nuclear deterrence can have on low intensity conflict, there is also the possibility that terrorists would be used as delivery systems for nuclear payloads outside the deterrence framework. This so-called "nexus effect" of rogue states, weapons of mass destruction and terror groups was the intellectual underpinning the decision to pursue regime change in Iraq.[20] The logic of the "nexus" is that it defeats deterrence by removing accountability from the equation. A country that cannot be held responsible for an offensive nuclear strike cannot be deterred; and nuclear retaliation is meaningless in the context of targeting a terrorist group, particularly one that idealizes martyrdom. Comparing Iran to Iraq on all three of the "nexus" pillars gives little cause for confidence. Iran has a definite desire and growing capability to develop nuclear weapons, a much less stable regime, and long-running links to international terrorist groups with global reach.

The notion of the nexus has been discounted by some who believe that no regime would place nuclear weapons into the hands of terrorists for fear of losing control of the weapons and perhaps having them used against other targets, or even against itself.[21] But it takes little imagination to formulate potential safeguards against misuse, such as arming codes or keys that would not be made available to the proxy group until the weapon is at the agreed-upon point and ready to be detonated. Yet, it is also possible that terrorist groups could obtain nuclear weapons through bribery or theft from Iran or similar less-developed countries with questionable nuclear security protocols. This possibility alone shows the destabilizing effect of nuclear weapons proliferation; humanity's most destructive weapons are gradually being placed in the care of governments of questionable reliability, prudence, and expertise. Whether the nexus scenario is activated by design or ineptitude, the results would be equally devastating.

The uncertainties introduced into the international system by the potential of a fully enabled "nexus" state in Iran led French President Jacques Chirac in early 2006 to declare in a speech that "leaders of states who would use terrorist means against us... must understand that they would lay themselves open to a firm and adapted response on our part."[22] In doing so, the French president was attempting to bring deterrence back into the strategic equation by threatening Iran (as was widely interpreted) before the fact. Essentially, Tehran (or other state sponsors) would be held responsible for any future WMD strikes on French soil by surrogate groups.

WHO IS DETERRED?

It must be noted that there is a preferable and more durable nuclear deterrence framework than that of Mutual Assured Destruction. It is one in which one party has nuclear weapons and the other does not. This favorable framework is in place right now, and in it the United States and other countries have the preponderance of power. It would be irrational for the U.S. and other established nuclear powers to help construct an alternative model in which all countries come closer to parity.

The issue at hand is not whether Iran will be deterred once it develops nuclear weapons. The more salient question is: to what extent will the rest of the world be deterred by a nuclear-armed Iran? There are scores of possible scenarios short of nuclear war that demonstrate that deterrence at the nuclear level does not automatically translate into stability at lower levels of conflict. In fact, it leads to permanent instability as regimes pursue conflict by other means, relying on their nuclear insurance cards to deter the U.S. or any other power from using decisive measures. Consciously allowing the Iranian regime to assume the mantle of a nuclear power, therefore, would be an act of catastrophic strategic negligence, and one that would make the world a much more dangerous place.

ENDNOTES

1. See, for example, Mario E. Carranza, "An Impossible Game: Stable Nuclear Deterrence after the Indian and Pakistani Tests," *Non-Proliferation Review* 6, no. 3 (1999), 11-24.

2. The unstated implication of this argument is that an Iranian nuclear capability would remove Israel's option to carry out a first strike. Hence the notion that this balance would be more stable.

3. Judith S. Yaphe and Charles D. Lutes, "Reassessing the Implications of a Nuclear-Armed Iran," National Defense University *McNair Paper* no. 69 (2005), xiii-xiv.

4. The case of North Korea, which has far fewer resources and exists in a more dire international situation, is another important example of a regime that does not accept the Western intellectual notion that nuclear weapons have little value.

5. See Lawrence Freedman, *Deterrence* (Cambridge: Policy Press, 2004), and Colin S. Gray, *Maintaining Effective Deterrence* (Carlisle, PA: Strategic Studies Institute, U.S. Army War College, 2003).

6. See, for example, Scott Peterson, "Waiting for the Rapture in Iran," *Christian Science Monitor*, December 21, 2005; see also Daniel Pipes, "The Mystical Menace of Mahmoud Ahmadinejad," *New York Sun*, January 10, 2006.

7. "Iran President Paves the Way for Arabs' Imam Return," Reuters, November 17, 2005.

8. See, for example, the argument presented in Gabi Avital, "End Nuclear Ambiguity: Israel Should Present Clear Second-Strike Capability in Face of Iranian Threat," *Yediot Ahronot* (Tel Aviv), October 18, 2006, http://www.ynetnews.com/articles/0,7340,L-3316491,00.html.

9. It should be noted that the United States withdrew from the agreement in 2002, with no ill effects.

10. See the *Memorandum of Understanding Regarding the Establishment of a Direct Communications Line* signed by the United States and the Soviet Union in June 20, 1963. The "hotline," originally a teletype system, was not actually used until the 1967 Arab-Israeli War.

11. Richard Beeston, "Six Arab States Join Rush to Go Nuclear," *Times of London*, November 4, 2006, http://www.timesonline.co.uk/article/0,,3-2436948,00.html. The states in question are Algeria, Egypt, Morocco, Tunisia, the UAE and Saudi Arabia.

12. Incidentally, the same equation can be argued with respect to North Korea. If Pyongyang attacked Seoul with nuclear weapons, would the United States respond and place cities from San Diego to Seattle at risk, especially for something that could not be undone?

[13.] On the Soviet global terror network, see Uri Ra'anan et al, eds., *Hydra of Carnage: International Linkages of Terrorism: The Witnesses Speak* (Lexington, MA: Lexington Books, 1986).

[14.] This is not to say that neither side planned to conduct nuclear conflict; rather, if such a conflict was to occur, it would be on its own merits, not as a consequence of a local conflict that spun out of control.

[15.] The Korean War also weighed heavily on the minds of decision-makers, particularly the prospect of Chinese conventional intervention and unacceptable casualty levels. However, this proved to be a poor bargain; the Vietnam War resulted in 73 percent more American deaths than the Korean conflict, and the United States failed to keep the Republic of Vietnam free.

[16.] Christopher Langton, ed., *The Military Balance 2006* (London: International Institute for Strategic Studies, 2006), 398, 399, 403. In 2004, Iran spent an estimated $5.6 billion on defense, while the United States spent $455.9 billion.

[17.] These scenarios are drawn from James S. Robbins, "Let Iran Go Nuclear?" *National Review Online*, January 10, 2006.

[18.] See Vasili Mitrokhin and Christopher Andrew, *The World Was Going Our Way: The KGB and the Battle for the Third World* (New York: Basic Books, 2005); See also Ra'anan et al, *Hydra of Carnage*.

[19.] Aaron Mannes, *Profiles in Terror: The Guide to Middle East Terrorist Organizations* (Lanham, MD: Rowman & Littlefield, 2004), 145-178.

[20.] Under Secretary of Defense for Policy Douglas J. Feith, "U.S. Strategy for the War on Terrorism," Speech before the Political Union of the University of Chicago, Chicago, Illinois, April 14, 2004.

[21.] See, for example, Yaphe and Lutes, xiv: "Many specialists on Iran share a widespread feeling that Iran's desire to be seen as a pragmatic nuclear power would tend to rein in whatever ideological impulses it might otherwise have to disseminate nuclear weapons or technologies to terrorists."

[22.] Molly Moore, "Chirac: Nuclear Response to Terrorism Is Possible," *Washington Post*, January 20, 2006, A12.

Getting Outreach Right

Robert A. Schadler, Bijan R. Kian
and Ilan Berman

Traditionally, Americans have been very bad at grand strategy. By contrast, they long have been very good at what is known as public diplomacy, usually without even trying. Over the years, the concept of "America" has captured the imagination of peoples around the world. Our remarkable history of peace and prosperity, and of political and economic freedom with relative social harmony, has been a beacon for great thinkers as well as illiterate peasants who simply want a better life for themselves and their children. This fascination with America—its ideals, institutions, mores and practices—has often compensated for our own chronic disability to conceive and carry out grand strategy.

The latter stages of the Cold War were a fortunate exception to this rule, because the adept use of public diplomacy became a major part of the overall grand strategy of the United States.[1] This achievement was all the more remarkable because the Cold War was not overwhelmingly military in character, and, therefore, needed subtlety and persistence in addition to bluntness and brute military strength. Its broad-ranging character and global dimensions made formulating a grand strategy that incorporated as many elements of national power as possible particularly difficult. Yet a robust public diplomacy effort that communicated with key publics within the Soviet Union was a central element (but by no means the only one) to successfully ending the Cold War without massive death and destruction. The Voice of America (VOA), Radio Liberty and Radio Free Europe—and the U.S. Information Agency overall—were among the heroes of that remarkable achievement.

But the successful demise of the Soviet Union brought out one of America's most charming characteristics: naïve optimism. When the U.S. no longer faces an obvious and immediate threat, its first inclination tends to be to dismantle much of the structures that allowed for its success. In 1929, the State Department dismantled all of its encryption capabilities, thinking that such efforts as deciphering cables of other countries were unworthy of gentlemen engaged in proper diplomacy.[2] After World War II, the Voice of America itself was on the verge of abolition.[3] After all, politicians asked at the time, why spend money on an agency that had first been called the "Office of War Information," even after the war was over?[4]

The end of the Cold War was no different. With the demise of the USSR, the mirage of a "peace dividend" again appeared. Some even spoke of the collapse of Soviet socialism ushering in the "end of history," when peace and prosperity—as well as democracy and capitalism—would spread to all corners of the earth.[5] For the field of public diplomacy, the outcome was earth-shaking; in 1999, the U.S. Information Agency, the parent agency of the VOA and Worldnet operations, was dismantled and merged into the Department of State. In its place, the current hybrid system for broadcast operations—part diplomatic and part bureaucratic—was created.

Few experts now dispute that this reconfiguration, carried out under the banner of "fiscal discipline," marked the beginning of today's dysfunctional public diplomacy. In retrospect, almost no one would look back on this bipartisan action as one that promoted effective public policy or the long-range national interest. America is simply too interesting, too successful, too prosperous, too energetic, too powerful and, overall, too significant to the rest of the world for the rest of the world not to want to understand it better. If we do not—consciously, deliberately and intelligently—communicate what is most important about us to them, they will rely heavily or entirely on what those who are ignorant or hostile say about us, in addition to the random and often crude caricatures that we export. Without proper public diplomacy, "Dallas" and "Desperate Housewives," Britney Spears and Eminem, rather than The Federalist Papers and the Bill of Rights, become the prisms through which the outside world views the United States.

This drift has not gone unnoticed. Since the dismantling of USIA, almost every important leader concerned with foreign policy, American or otherwise, has lamented the poor state of U.S. public diplomacy.[6] Some have gone so far as to call it dysfunctional.[7] They have good reason for doing so; over the past seven years, a great many talented people have left government altogether. Those who remain have been dispersed throughout the bureaucracy, diluting the incredible "talent pool" that was created during the Reagan years. The results speak for themselves. Instead of a coherent agency with a billion-dollar budget and ten thousand employees worldwide, we have occasional, nice-sounding, newsworthy initiatives announced with great fanfare, while broadcasts to key countries and essential social outreach programs have been eliminated in their entirety.

PUBLIC DIPLOMACY ADRIFT

The enduring paradox is that this transformation has taken place at the time when a coordinated, clear public diplomacy effort has become more important than ever. Even in a time of relative concord, it still is necessary to speak to foreign audiences about what the United States stands for, why it is what is and why it does what it does. Today, in a time of conflict, nothing is more crucial. And in this struggle for hearts and minds, there is no more important battlefield than the Islamic Republic of Iran, the ideological and political epicenter of global Shi'a Islam.

To its credit, the Bush administration has belatedly taken notice of this fact. In February 2006, Secretary of State Condoleezza Rice articulated what amounted to a sea change in U.S. policy toward Iran when she appeared before the Senate Foreign Relations Committee to request $75 million in supplemental funds for Iran-related programming. "The United States will actively confront the aggressive policies of this Iranian regime," Rice confirmed to lawmakers. "And at the same time, we are going to work to support the aspirations of the Iranian people for freedom in their own country."[8] The goals of the White House are ambitious:

- To increase U.S. government broadcasting into Iran through the establishment of a new 24/7 Farsi-language channel into Iran, as well as upgrades to radio transmission capabilities and investments in satellite broadcasting technology for existing radio and television programming;

- To promote democratic processes within Iran, specifically, to "foster participation in the political process and support efforts to expand internet access as a tool for civic organization," with the help of groups like the National Endowment for Democracy, the National Democratic Institute and the International Republican Institute;

- To provide educational opportunities to young Iranians through scholarships and international visitors programs, and

- To bolster Internet outreach to Iran, as well as provide support to independent Farsi-language television and radio outlets.[9]

As a practical matter, however, little has changed. More than five years into the War on Terror, American public outreach continues to suffer from deep systemic dysfunctions.

The most glaring has to do with corporate culture. The U.S. government's replacement for the USIA's oversight of international broadcasting is an appointed bipartisan board known as the Broadcasting Board of Governors (BBG). But, unlike its predecessor, the BBG is not well positioned to provide a single, coherent vision of how broadcasting needs to fit into an overall public diplomacy strategy. Its members are overwhelmingly successful businessmen and women who still maintain roots in the private sector. As a result, a corporate mentality permeates Board activities. As one member, Edward Kaufman, put it, "We've got to think of ourselves as separate from public diplomacy."[10] Yet another, Norman Pattiz, famously remarked that it was his belief that it was MTV, rather than American ideals or Soviet corruption, "that brought down the Berlin Wall."[11] The result has been predictable: a downplaying, if not an outright dismissal, of the distinguishing governmental purpose—promoting American ideals—in favor of an emphasis on gaining "audience share." Governmental oversight, meanwhile, has been lax, with only sporadic Cabinet-level attention and little input regarding programming and content.

Given this state of affairs, it is perhaps not surprising that the Board has molded itself into an entity independent from, and occasionally directly opposed to, governmental policy. Evidence of this rot became painfully apparent in late 2005, when the Board commissioned the global consulting group Booz Allen Hamilton to conduct a top-down review of its management style. The resulting study, presented to the BBG in January of 2006, slammed the BBG for multiple failures in corporate governance, including micromanagement and lack of accountability, and recommended the separation of management from the day-to-day workings of the Voice of America and other public diplomacy outlets.[12] The BBG's response, however, was not reform but suppression. And, after substantial political pressure from the Board, Booz Allen revised the report, re-issuing a "scrubbed" version that omitted the offending passages and prescriptions.[13]

Just as problematic, however, are the deficiencies in current broadcasting content. True to the BBG's corporate ethos, U.S. government broadcasting toward Iran has been well and truly "MTV-ified." Hard-hitting political analysis and coverage of current events currently account for one-third or less of the regular programming on Radio Free Europe's 24-hour broadcast outlet, Radio Farda, with the remaining airtime taken up by lengthy broadcasts of popular music.[14] Such a schedule is clearly designed to appeal to Iran's young, Western-oriented population, but does so at the expense of a robust U.S. democratic message. Farda's television counterpart, the Voice of America, meanwhile, operates on a much more limited schedule, airing just three hours of broadcasting daily. Yet even these broadcasts rely upon "filler" content from such outlets as CNN to supplement its original news programming.[15]

Even the meaningful content that does come through ends up being substantially diluted. A recent study commissioned by the U.S. government's Iran Steering Group, jointly chaired by the State Department and the National Security Council, found that the main instruments of official U.S. broadcasting into Iran "both fall short of realizing their stated mission and mandate." That study cites several problems endemic to both the Voice of America and Radio Farda, including self-censorship in the selection of content, inadequate analysis and interpretation of important events, poor context for events that are interpreted, and an overwhelming emphasis on journalistic "balance," often at the expense of a proper framing of issues.[16]

The results are unmistakable. "Balanced" though it may be, when it comes to Iran our current outreach is neither appropriate nor effective. Even though it consumes millions of taxpayer dollars annually, and despite the fact that Voice of America and Radio Farda do indeed appear to have substantial audiences, U.S. broadcasting toward Iran is at best "reactive," rather than proactive. At worst, it is downright damaging to American objectives and values.

SETTING THE AGENDA

Reversing course requires the United States to make major investments in a number of areas. Chief among them is clarity of purpose. Today, VOA officials can be accused of being off-message when they make clear that they are "not in the business of persuading Iranians to overthrow their government."[17] It cannot be said, however, that they are actively subverting American policy. Rather, the current disarray in the implementation of U.S. broadcasting is attributable at least partly to a lack of clear direction from the country's political leadership. Simply put, the U.S. government must definitively decide whether it simply wants to modify the behavior of Iran's ayatollahs, or to seek a more fundamental political transformation in Tehran. Once it does so, it will need to enforce that preference at both a bureaucratic and a programmatic level throughout the entire U.S. public diplomacy bureaucracy.

This change, moreover, must be reflected in the quality of the actual content that is generated by U.S. broadcasting. Today, U.S. outreach has degenerated into prolonged sessions of entertainment, often carried out at the expense of proven approaches to shaping the strategic landscape through cultural, intellectual and historical programming. And the audience has taken notice; anecdotal evidence suggests that although American radio—and to a lesser degree, television—broadcasts are ubiquitous throughout the Islamic Republic, they desperately need a reconfiguration that provides for greater discourse about liberal Western democracy, personal freedoms and political independence.[18] Key themes requiring amplification include: American support for political opposition forces within Iran; the fallacy of the Iranian regime as the sole source of Islamic knowledge; the corruption endemic to the country's ruling clerical class; and the dangers that the Iranian regime's quest for nuclear weapons poses to its own population.

To be successful, however, such a transformation will require Washington to make its outreach more adaptive. Since taking office in August 2005, Iranian President Mahmoud Ahmadinejad has spearheaded a systematic assault on media freedoms within the Islamic Republic in an effort to eradicate "Western influence" from Iranian society. This campaign has included major new restrictions on radio, television and film content, a ban on the publication of virtually all books within the country, and serious incidents of media intimidation directed against opposition journalists, among other measures. Current American outreach is deeply susceptible to such pressure, since VOA Persian and Radio Farda both utilize media (radio and television) that are among the most likely to be adversely affected by the Iranian regime's widening crackdown.

By contrast, other media, chief among them the Internet, are far less vulnerable. Currently, the number of Internet users in Iran is estimated at more than five million, roughly eight percent of the country's population, making the Islamic Republic one of the most "wired" nations in the Third World. This constituency, moreover, is expected to expand to as many as 25 million users (over 35 percent of the population) by the end of the decade.[19] This remarkable growth has led the Iranian regime to impose extensive restrictions on Internet usage and content. According to the OpenNet Initiative, a joint project of the University of Toronto, the Harvard University Law School, Cambridge University and Oxford University, the Iranian regime "is among a small group of states with the most sophisticated state-mandated filtering systems in the world."[20] Yet encouraging signs suggest that even these harsh restrictions increasingly have failed to keep pace with Internet usage and access on the part of the Iranian people, making web-based communications among the most important forms of "new media" available to the United States *vis-à-vis* Iran. By using advanced Internet techniques (podcasts, email blasts, newsgroup postings and secondary distribution), and by adapting delivery strategies to exploit vulnerabilities in the Iranian regime's control of the media, it will be possible to continue to deliver necessary information to Iranian activists for the foreseeable future, in spite of the increasingly sophisticated media filters and restrictions imposed by the Islamic Republic.

None of this can be accomplished without proper resources, however, and American outreach toward Iran remains woefully underfunded. In 2004, broadcasting to Iran accounted for about two-and-a-half percent of the BBG's total $577 million budget, and just over one percent of the U.S. government's combined $1.17 billion public diplomacy budget.[21] While the Bush administration's February 2006 funding request aims to increase the amount spent on broadcasting to Iran considerably, projected funding levels still fall far short of what is needed to properly address Iran's geopolitical importance, or the technical hurdles (linguistic, cultural and operational) that accompany such outreach. The U.S. government must further expand its financial investment in public broadcasting toward Iran in order to make it commensurate with the magnitude of the challenge to American interests now posed by the Iranian regime.

At the same time, it needs to make better use of an important ally: the Iranian diaspora. Currently, expatriate outreach to the Iranian people far outstrips official U.S. government broadcasting, encompassing a dozen or more television stations and one radio station that broadcast into the Islamic Republic via satellite and the Internet. These outlets, moreover, have achieved measurable successes, garnering significant public awareness inside Iran. Yet for years, they have scraped along on shoestring budgets without any sort of official support from the U.S. government, leaving them vulnerable to economic and political pressure from the regime in Tehran. And little has changed: even now, government priorities overwhelmingly favor official broadcasting outlets, allocating some $50 million to the expansion of Radio Farda and VOA programming, and just $5 million to expatriate radio and television stations.[22] Such assistance is certainly welcome, but it fails to appreciate the potential contribution expatriate broadcasting can make to public diplomacy toward Iran. American officials must make it a priority to supplement existing official programming with the requisite funds to truly empower such private sector efforts.

Finally, when it comes to Iran, broadcasting looms especially large as a communications vehicle, both because of the lack of official contacts between the U.S. and the Islamic Republic and because of the sophistication of the target audience. But public diplomacy is much broader than simply radio and television programming; it should include scholarships, fellowships, speeches, artistic performances and a wide array of face-to-face meetings and exchanges, among numerous other efforts. Yet such complimentary initiatives—gutted during the 1990s as part of the elusive "peace dividend" sought by American officials—remain extremely underdeveloped. Between 1991 and 2001, the number of academic and cultural exchanges between the United States and foreign nations was slashed by nearly 40 percent (from 45,000 to 29,000 annually) and the profile of American information centers abroad scaled down dramatically.[23] The results have been pronounced; without such grassroots contacts, Washington has been unable to effectively counteract the negative media image of America in the Arab and Islamic worlds. Even more significantly, this constriction has prevented the United States from properly identifying and engaging emerging pro-democracy leaders in the region—a key ingredient of American successes against the Soviet Union during the Cold War.

Such mechanisms are especially vital in the case of Iran, because its population is overwhelmingly young, culturally sophisticated and Western-looking. It is, therefore, encouraging that the Bush administration has begun to focus in that area, requesting $15 million for civil society work within Iran and $5 million for scholarships for young Iranians to come and study in the United States.[24] At the same time, it has quietly encouraged programs and initiatives in third countries that are designed to train and empower Iranian civic leaders in their opposition to the regime in Tehran.[25] These initial steps need to be strengthened and expanded as a way of harnessing the political currents now visible on the Iranian "street."

THE STAKES

Washington has a great deal riding on this effort. The Islamic Republic of Iran has emerged as a key intellectual battlefield in the Global War on Terror. Iran's vibrant, youthful population (some 45 million people aged 35 or younger) represents an indispensable constituency in the "battle of ideas" that is now taking place in the greater Middle East. For, irrespective of what happens in the near future (on the nuclear front or any other), a decade-and-a-half hence it will be this public—rather than the country's current sclerotic clerical leadership—that will rule Iran.

By recalibrating its outreach toward Iran, the United States has the ability to better engage this group, and to stimulate a debate within it about the costs of continuing down the current political path, more positive alternative futures, and exactly what is required to achieve them. Just as easily, however, Washington can preserve its current public diplomacy drift, muting its support for human rights and democratic change within Iran. By doing so, however, it will risk forfeiting the ability to positively influence the country's political direction—and, by extension, its attitudes toward the United States. For a country that has publicly declared its commitment to promoting "a balance of power that favors freedom,"[26] the choice should be an easy one to make.

ENDNOTES

1. *National Security Decision Directive 75*, signed by President Reagan on January 17, 1983 is a preeminent example of the connection of public diplomacy to an overall strategy.

2. See Herbert O. Yardley, *The American Black Chamber* (Indianapolis: Bobbs-Merrill, 1931).

3. James L. Tyson, *U.S. International Broadcasting and National Security* (New York: Ramapo Press, 1983), 4.

4. "On August 31, 1945 [President Truman] also promulgated an executive order terminating the OWI... Their functions were transferred to an Interim International Information Service, which was supposed to dismantle itself by the end of the year." Ibid., 7; see also Robert W. Pirsein, *The Voice of America—A History of International Broadcasting Activities of the United States Government, 1940-1962* (New York: Arno Press, 1979.)

5. Francis Fukuyama, *The End of History and the Last Man* (New York: Harper Perennial, 1993).

6. See, for example, Vice President Dick Cheney, as cited in Jim VandeHei, "Cheney Defends Bush Appointments," *Washington Post*, March 23, 2005, and former Defense Secretary Donald Rumsfeld, as cited in Al Kamen, "Make Haste For Baghdad," *Washington Post*, June 15, 2005.

7. See, for example, Senator Richard Lugar, as cited in Richard Wolffe and Holly Bailey, "The Price of an Ambassadorship," newsweek.com, July 27, 2006, http://www.msnbc.msn.com/id/8730875/site/newsweek/.

8. Condoleezza Rice, Remarks before the Senate Foreign Relations Committee, February 15, 2006, http://www.state.gov/secretary/rm/2006/61262.htm.

9. Ibid.

10. As cited in Glenn Hauser, ed., *DX Listening Digest* 2-142, September 11, 2002, http://www.worldofradio.com/dxld2142.txt.

11. As cited in "The Sound of America," *New Yorker*, February 18 and 25, 2002, http://www.newyorker.com/talk/content/articles/020218ta_talk_mayer.

12. Booz Allen Hamilton, "Draft Report to the Board: Review of the Voice of America and the International Broadcasting Bureau, Broadcasting Board of Governors," January 11, 2006, 49, 51, 65. (authors' collection)

13. Booz Allen Hamilton, "Final Report – Volume 1: Review of the Voice of America and the International Broadcasting Bureau, Broadcasting Board of Governors," July 2006, http://www.technewslit.com/USIAAA/BAH_Vol_1.pdf.

14. "DRAFT: A Study of USG Broadcasting into Iran Prepared for the Iran Steering Group," U.S. Department of Defense, Office of the Secretary of Defense, September 14, 2006, 1. (authors' collection)

15. Ibid.

16. Ibidem.

17. Former VOA Director David Jackson, as cited in Guy Dinmore, "US Hails the Iranian People But Not Their 'Lunatic' Leaders," *Financial Times* (London), May 23, 2006, http://www.ft.com/cms/s/866h2cfe-ea12-11da-a33b-0000779e2340.html.

18. "DRAFT: A Study of USG Broadcasting into Iran Prepared for the Iran Steering Group," 1.

19. All statistics derived from OpenNet Initiative, *Internet Filtering in Iran in 2004-2005: A Country Study*, June 2005, available online at http://www.opennetinitiative.net/studies/iran/ONI_Country_Study_Iran.pdf.

20. Ibid.

21. Extrapolated from Broadcasting Board of Governors, *Broadcasting to Iran Fact Sheet*, June 16, 2003 and Broadcasting Board of Governors, *BBG Broadcasting to Iran*, January 4, 2005.

22. Ibid.

23. Stephen Johnson and Helle Dale, "How to Reinvigorate U.S. Public Diplomacy," Heritage Foundation *Backgrounder* no. 1645, April 2003, 4.

24. Rice, Remarks before the Senate Foreign Relations Committee.

25. Guy Dinmore, "Bush Enters Debate on Freedom in Iran," *Financial Times*, March 30, 2006, http://www.ft.com/cms/s/364cda0e-c016-11da-939f-0000779e2340.html.

26. White House, Office of the Press Secretary, *National Security Strategy of the United States of America*, September 2002, 29.

THE ECONOMICS OF CONFRONTING IRAN

Ilan Berman

Addressing the Johns Hopkins University's prestigious Nitze School of Advanced International Studies in November 2005, the State Department's chief policy planner staked out a series of exceedingly ambitious American policy goals toward Iran.[1] "In coordination with our allies, U.S. policy strives to isolate Iran, promote a diplomatic solution to Iran's nuclear ambitions, expose and oppose the regime's support for terrorism, and advance the cause of democracy and human rights within Iran itself," Undersecretary of State for Political Affairs Nicholas Burns told the assembled audience. Doing so, Burns made clear, is at least in part an economic exercise. "Through its diplomatic contacts and its trade and investment, the world does have leverage—and that leverage should be used constructively now—to convince the hard-liners in Tehran that there is a price for their misguided policies."[2]

In practice, however, neither Washington nor its international allies have yet seriously tackled the economic dimension of the current crisis with Iran—or explored the financial levers by which the Islamic Republic can be confronted. This state of affairs is surprising, given the formidable arsenal of economic tools that are currently available to the West. Thankfully, it is also reversible; the United States and the international community today have the ability to marshal an extensive array of economic approaches in order to contain and confront the Iranian regime.

WHAT FUELS IRANIAN INTRANSIGENCE?

More than any other factor, Iran's defiance in its current stand-off with the West has been made possible by energy. Over the past several years, the Islamic Republic has emerged as a *bona fide* energy superpower. Home to approximately 10 percent of world oil, Iran is the second largest exporter in the Organization of Petroleum Exporting Countries (OPEC), producing an average of 3.9 million barrels of oil per day. At the same time, Iran sits atop the world's second-largest reserves of natural gas (some 940 trillion cubic feet). As a result, Iran's economy is overwhelmingly energy-based. Today, the vast majority (80 to 90 percent) of Iran's export earnings, as well as about one half of its budget and a quarter of its gross domestic product, is derived from energy exports to the international community.[3]

In the past, this energy-dominated economy has led to wild fluctuations in Iran's financial fortunes. During the late 1990s, plummeting world oil prices left the Iranian regime nearly bankrupt.[4] Today, however, quite the opposite is true; the rising price of world oil generated by political instability associated with the War on Terror has provided Iran with a staggering fiscal windfall. As of March 2006 (the end of Iranian calendar year 1384), officials in Tehran were publicly estimating their country's hard currency reserves at some $50 billion.[5] A similar figure is projected for Iranian oil revenues in 2006-2007.[6] These added resources and financial cushion can be expected to dramatically increase the Iranian regime's willingness to engage in risky regional behavior, as well as to accelerate the pace and scope of its strategic programs, in the months and years to come.

Iranian officials have attempted to solidify this economic status through a major expansion of their country's international energy profile. Over the past three years, Iran signed two massive exploration and development accords, worth an estimated $100 billion over the next twenty-five years, with China alone.[7] A growing number of other nations, including France, Malaysia, Japan, Canada, and Italy, are now engaged in the development of existing oil fields within the country, and this involvement is expected to increase as recent discoveries—including the Azadegan field and Bangestan reservoirs in southern Iran, as well as the offshore Dasht-e-Abadan site near the southwestern port city of Abadan—begin to come online.

Iran also has commenced efforts to become a major global exporter of natural gas. Since 2002, it supplies Turkey with substantial natural gas deliveries via a bilateral pipeline link and, according to official Turkish government statistics, could provide roughly 20 percent of total Turkish natural gas consumption by the end of the decade.[8]

A similar arrangement is emerging between Iran and Armenia as part of a pipeline, currently under construction, that could supply Armenia with up to 47 billion cubic meters over a period of 20 to 25 years, beginning in 2007.[9] Iran has opened similar discussions with Georgia, and has even taken steps to coordinate natural gas policy with Moscow as part of a Russia-led natural gas cartel now emerging in the "post-Soviet space."[10]

At the same time, the Iranian regime has dramatically increased its ability to leverage its strategic location in the Strait of Hormuz, the principal passageway for roughly two-fifths of world oil trade. According to U.S. intelligence estimates, a sustained national military rearmament over the past several years now provides Iran with the ability to temporarily shut off the flow of oil from the Persian Gulf, even with a Western military presence in the region.[11]

It is a testament to this energy clout that, as the international crisis over Iran's runaway nuclear ambitions has deepened, Iranian officials have repeatedly raised the specter of a disruption of energy trade in the Persian Gulf. Regime officials such as Mohammed-Nabi Rudaki, deputy chairman of the Iranian parliament's national security committee, have warned that the Islamic Republic has the power to "to halt oil supply to the last drop from the shores of the Persian Gulf via the Straits of Hormuz" should serious measures be undertaken against the Islamic Republic at the United Nations.[12] Similarly, Iranian president Mahmoud Ahmadinejad has warned the United States and Europe that the global price of crude has not yet reached its "real value."[13] Even Iran's Supreme Leader, the Ayatollah Ali Khamenei, has threatened the West with disruptions in fuel shipments from the Persian Gulf in the event of a "wrong move" against Iran.[14] And regime officials have concretely demonstrated their capacity to do so, holding multiple aerial, naval and ground maneuvers in the Persian Gulf in recent months to showcase the force-projection capabilities of their elite clerical army, the Pasdaran.

ASSESSING IRANIAN VULNERABILITIES

Given such posturing, it is not surprising that some analysts have concluded that energy is Iran's "trump card" in its dealings with the West.[15] However, closer examination suggests that—notwithstanding its obvious energy power—Iran's economy is far from healthy. In fact, the Islamic Republic is deeply susceptible to economic pressure from the international community on a number of fronts.

Petroleum products

Despite its massive oil production (some 3.9 million barrels daily), Iran is a voracious consumer of foreign gasoline. The Islamic Republic imports more than a third of its annual consumption of over 64.5 million liters from a variety of foreign sources[16] at an estimated cost of more than $3 billion annually.[17] These imports are not surplus; Iran reportedly maintains just 45 days worth of gasoline domestically, and requires steady supplies of refined petroleum products from abroad for the continued functioning of its economy.[18] At the same time, the Islamic Republic's antiquated socialist economic practices preserve deep state subsidies on the domestic price of gasoline; current costs per gallon hover at under 40 cents.[19]

Gasoline imports, therefore, are an enormous drag on the Iranian economy. In mid-2006, leading Iranian policymakers predicted that the regime would need to spend an extra $5 billion (fully 10 percent of its amassed hard currency reserves) that year alone to maintain state subsidies avoid domestic rationing.[20] Costs for the Iranian fiscal year ending March 2007 are expected to be similarly high—nearly $7 billion in regime funds to defray the high cost of gasoline to Iranian consumers.[21] Regime efforts to minimize this economic vulnerability, meanwhile, lag behind the times; although Iranian officials—with foreign assistance—have launched a major effort to expand indigenous gasoline production,[22] a substantial decline in Iran's dependence on foreign petroleum is not expected until at least the end of the decade. This state of affairs has led knowledgeable observers to conclude that Iran is facing what amounts to a "gasoline time bomb."[23]

As such, the imposition of a comprehensive embargo on foreign gasoline supplies to Iran could achieve rapid and significant results. The immediate effects would be a depletion of hard currency reserves as the regime scrambles to secure new sources of gasoline to replace lost suppliers, as well as potentially serious work stoppages in "gasoline heavy" industrial sectors such as shipping. However, if robust and sustained for long enough, a gasoline embargo has the power to impact the stability of the Iranian regime itself. Because of the nature of its economic construct, the Iranian regime is limited in the ways that it can respond to such economic pressure. Essentially, policymakers in Tehran will have just two choices, to raise the price of gasoline at the domestic pump or begin petroleum rationing, each of which carries the potential to generate widespread social unrest.

Centralized economic hierarchy

Today, the vast majority of regime wealth is concentrated in the hands of a small group of people, whose associates and relatives dominate the Iranian

---

economy. The most public of these is the extended family of former Iranian president (and current Expediency Council chairman) Ali Akbar Hashemi Rafsanjani, which now virtually controls copper mining in Iran, the regime's lucrative pistachio trade, and a number of profitable industrial and export-import businesses.[24] Rafsanjani alone is believed to have amassed a personal fortune of close to $2 billion, largely by obtaining—and then failing to repay—loans from the country's state-owned banks.[25]

A related economic power center is Iran's *bonyads*, the sprawling, largely-unregulated religious/social foundations overseen by Iran's Supreme Leader. Arguably the most important of these is the *Bonyad-e Mostazafan* (Foundation of the Oppressed), a complex network of an estimated 1,200 firms created in 1979 with seed money from the Shah's coffers.[26] Another is the *Bonyad-e Shahid*, a colossal conglomerate of industrial, agricultural, construction and commercial companies with some 350 offices and tens of thousands of employees.[27] The sums controlled by these organs are enormous; the *Bonyad-e Mostazafan* alone was known in 1995 to command some $3 billion. That number today is believed to be closer to $11 billion.[28] In all, *bonyads* are estimated to control more than 30 percent of Iran's national GDP (and as much as two-thirds of the country's non-oil GDP).[29]

Given this economic hierarchy, targeted financial measures that restrict the ability of these individuals and organizations to access international markets—and curtail their capacity to engage in commerce—are likely to have an immediate and pronounced effect on regime decision-making.

Foreign direct investment

Iran may currently be experiencing a financial windfall as a result of the high price of world oil, but the dozens of billions of surplus dollars collected by the Iranian government over the past several years have done little to diminish Iran's need for foreign direct investment. According to authoritative estimates, Iran's energy sector still requires some $1 billion annually to maintain current production levels, and $1.5 billion a year to increase this capacity.[30] Moreover, without such sustained capital, it is believed that Iran could revert from an energy powerhouse to a net energy importer in the span of very few years.[31]

As a result, multilateral measures that target foreign investment into Iran—and which curtail the relevant technology available to the Iranian regime—can help to slow Iran's nuclear progress, complicating Iran's access to foreign funding and/or forcing a further depletion of the hard currency reserves amassed by the regime over the past several years.

Moreover, history has shown that the effectiveness of sanctions can be enhanced by the speed and scope with which they are applied.[32] If coupled with effective public diplomacy, such measures also can drive a wedge between the Iranian government and its people over the prudence of nuclear acquisition. Nevertheless, given the scope of current foreign investment in Iran, it is unrealistic for the U.S. and its allies to expect to be able to achieve its comprehensive economic isolation.

Social indicators

When a relative political unknown named Mahmoud Ahmadinejad unexpectedly won the Iranian presidency in the country's summer 2005 elections, it was a telling indicator of the degree of domestic discontent with widespread economic inequalities within the Islamic Republic. Ahmadinejad's populist anti-corruption campaign, which pledged wider economic dividends for ordinary Iranians, stood in stark contrast to that of his opponent, former president Ali Akbar Hashemi Rafsanjani, widely recognized as one of the richest and most corrupt men in Iran. The results were predictable; a sweeping electoral victory for Ahmadinejad.

Yet more than a year into his presidency, Ahmadinejad's economic promises so far have failed to materialize. While the Iranian regime reports the national rate of inflation to be just over 10 percent, unofficial estimates place this figure significantly higher—at 15 percent or more.[33] Moreover, rampant spending by Ahmadinejad's government appears to be responsible for steady upward inflationary pressure.[34] Unemployment, meanwhile, remains widespread, with some thirty percent of the country's working-age population without gainful employment.[35] If implemented by the United States and its international partners, economic measures that exacerbate these internal conditions (by raising the internal rate of inflation, prompting abrupt commodity price hikes, or sparking commercial shortages) have the ability to exploit the existing fissures between the Iranian regime and its people, and to galvanize greater internal opposition to government practices.

Trade relationships

Today, Iran boasts a combined total foreign trade of over $52 billion dollars annually.[36] The regime's largest trading partners are Japan, China and the United Arab Emirates, which cumulatively account for over a fifth of Iran's total annual global trade.[37] Iranian officials have put a premium upon expanding their country's economic relations with existing partners, and establishing economic ties with new ones (particularly among the countries of the "post-Soviet space"). These nations' trade with Iran, how-ever, is dwarfed by their trade with the U.S. For example, Japan's annual two-way trade of $180 billion with the United States far outstrips its yearly turnover with Iran (some $3.7 billion).[38]

To be sure, this disparity has been the subject of U.S. attention for some time. For over a decade, through key pieces of legislation such as the 1996 Iran-Libya Sanctions Act—and more recently the Iran Freedom Support Act of 2006—the U.S. Congress has attempted to curb Iran's "ability to support acts of international terrorism and to fund the development and acquisition of weapons of mass destruction and the means to deliver them."[39] But so far, such measures have lain largely dormant and unused, neglected by an Executive Branch fearful of the likely negative repercussions on America's bilateral ties to nations that would be affected.[40]

This constitutes a major miscalculation; "second tier" sanctions are a critical tool in the U.S. economic arsenal *vis-à-vis* Iran. Simply put, continued commerce with an increasingly intransigent Iranian regime cannot continue to be perceived as "cost free" by the international community. By enacting—and then *actively enforcing*—such measures, policymakers in Washington have the ability to force Iran's trading partners to choose between doing business with Iran and conducting commerce with the United States, and to provide them with the political rationale necessary to make the proper choice.

For American policymakers, choosing which of these measures to employ will depend greatly upon the desired outcome of their policy. If Washington's main objective is simply to prod Iran back to the nuclear negotiating table, judicious use of measures such as multilateral and/or "smart" sanctions alone may have the desired effect—at least for a time. Such economic pressure, however, cannot diminish the Iranian regime's desire for the bomb, only help to delay its acquisition. If, however, the United States is serious about diminishing the overall international threat posed by Tehran, as well as sparking a fundamental political transformation within its borders, the use of more serious economic measures undoubtedly will be necessary.

A CLOSING WINDOW OF OPPORTUNITY

So far, the United States has been slow to truly capitalize upon Iran's economic vulnerabilities. Rather, the Bush administration has thrown its weight behind a slow-moving, convoluted diplomatic effort to coerce Iran to abandon its nuclear ambitions via the United Nations. By now, however, it is abundantly clear that this approach is not only suboptimal, but potentially downright dangerous.

The protracted diplomatic wrangling at the United Nations already has had a major deleterious effect. As of this writing, UN deliberations—underway since Iran's flouting of a late August 2006 deadline for a freeze on uranium enrichment—remain deadlocked, largely because of disagreements between the Permanent Members of the Security Council over the scope and severity of the measures to be applied. This inaction has provided Iran with valuable time to forge ahead with its nuclear effort.

Moreover, if and when United Nations sanctions do materialize, they are likely to be deeply influenced by politics. Since two of Iran's major strategic partners—Russia and China—wield veto power over Security Council action against Iran, any measures that emerge from UN deliberations are guaranteed to be limited in scope, so as not to offend either Moscow or Beijing. As such, they likely will not offend the Iranian regime much either.

Tehran, meanwhile, is capitalizing upon these realities. Over the past year, the Iranian regime has launched a major effort to limit its economic vulnerabilities. This includes large-scale transfers of assets from sanctions-prone European banks to more secure financial institutions in China and Southeast Asia.[41] Iran also initiated a major privatization of governmental funds, shuffling regime currency into private (and less easily traceable) hands.[42] Potentially most significant, Iran's parliament approved a fiscal budget calling for a halt to imports of refined petroleum products and the institution of gasoline rationing,[43] although such measures as yet do not appear to have come into effect.

The goal behind all of these efforts is crystal clear: to limit potential Western economic leverage over Iranian behavior. And, should Iran continue to make major progress toward this goal, it will become much harder than it is today to successfully apply economic pressure.

THE LIMITS OF IRANIAN OIL POWER

Today, it is clear that Iran has the ability to exert a high price from the international community if it is stymied in its nuclear efforts. But political and economic realities suggest that Iran's oil power is far more limited than commonly understood.

Iran could indeed curb oil exports, as regime officials have repeatedly threatened to do. However, if the Islamic Republic withdraws oil from world markets, it could face the prospect of losing much-needed business, as energy-hungry states are forced to quickly seek replacement suppliers. Moreover, the resulting perceptions that Iran is an "unreliable" energy partner are likely to reduce foreign direct investment flowing into the country—thereby placing Iran's current status as a global energy player in jeopardy.[44]

By the same token, a cut-off of oil exports is likely to reverse Iran's recent political gains abroad. Simply put, if Iran's energy brinksmanship has a negative effect on the economies of its political allies, those countries are far less likely to unconditionally support Iran on the perceived source of the economic turbulence: Iran's nuclear program. This change will be true in spades for major investors into Iran's energy sector (such as Japan, China and France).

Most of all, Iranian officials—despite official bluster—understand that actual use of the "oil weapon" is likely to have dire consequences for the stability and longevity of their regime. The international community's current diplomatic overtures toward Tehran have been generated in no small part by problems in attaining consensus on more robust measures. Substantial Iranian interference with the global energy market has the ability to change all that, galvanizing a serious consensus for aggressive containment—or even regime change—on the part of numerous energy-hungry nations. Iran's use of its "oil weapon," in other words, could prove fatal to the regime.

Is there a guarantee that sanctions will succeed in altering Iranian behavior and curbing its nuclear efforts? The answer is no. On the contrary, American policymakers should refrain from seeing economic sanctions as an isolated measure; historically, a strong correlation exists between the imposition of sanctions and the subsequent escalation to the use of force (e.g., Panama in 1989, Iraq in 1991, and the Balkans during the mid-1990s). What is clear, however, is that a failure by the international community to promptly utilize its existing economic leverage *vis-à-vis* Iran will make other, less attractive solutions—chief among them the use of force—much more likely.

Ultimately, the United States has a fundamental choice to make. Is it, and the world, willing to pay the political and economic price associated with a serious strategy to confront Iran? The alternative is to internalize a permanent hike in the cost of doing business with a region that will be dominated by an atomic Islamic Republic.

Endnotes

1. This chapter is expanded from testimony delivered by the author before the Joint Economic Committee of the United States Congress on July 25, 2006.

2. Undersecretary of State Nicholas Burns, "U.S. Policy Toward Iran," Remarks before the Johns Hopkins University Paul H. Nitze School of Advanced International Studies, Washington, DC, November 30, 2005, http://www.state.gov/p/us/rm/2005/57473.htm.

3. Energy Information Administration, United States Department of Energy, "Country Analysis Brief: Iran," April 2004, http://www.eia.doe.gov/emeu/cabs/iran.html.

4. See, for example, Michael Rubin, "What Are Iran's Domestic Priorities?" *Middle East Review of International Affairs* 6, no. 2 (2002), 26-27.

5. *Aftab-e Yazd* (Tehran), May 10, 2006, as translated in *Mideastwire Daily Briefing*, May 12, 2006, http://www.mideastwire.com.

6. "Iran Sees Oil Income of $54 Billion in 2006/07 – Paper," Rueters, July 9, 2006.

7. Robin Wright, "Iran's New Alliance with China Could Cost U.S. Leverage," *Washington Post*, November 17, 2004, A21.

8. "Turkish Energy Policy," Turkish Ministry of Foreign Affairs, n.d., http://www.mfa.gov.tr/grupa/an/policy.htm.

9. "Iran, Armenia Sign Agreement on Gas Export," *Asia Pulse*, May 18, 2004.

10. "Russia Favors Iran Route for Crude Exports," *Tehran Times*, June 14, 2004.

11. Defense Intelligence Agency Director Lowell E. Jacoby, "Current and Projected National Security Threats to the United States," Statement before the U.S. Senate Select Committee on Intelligence, February 16, 2005, http://intelligence.senate.gov/0502hrg/050216/jacoby.pdf.

12. Yossi Melman, "Iranian official: UN Sanctions May Lead Us to Seal Off Persian Gulf," *Ha'aretz* (Tel Aviv), January 24, 2006, http://www.haaretz.com/hasen/spages/674159.html.

13. "Iran: Oil Undervalued," United Press International, April 20, 2006.

14. "Tehran Warns of Fuel Disruptions," BBC (London), June 4, 2006, http://news.bbc.co.uk/2/hi/middle_east/5045604.stm.

15. See, for example, Clifford Kupchan, "Tehran's Trump Card," *Los Angeles Times*, April 23, 2006, http://www.latimes.com/news/printedition/suncommentary/la-op-kupchan23apr23,1,4489060.story?coll=la-headlines-suncomment.

16. These include the Persian Gulf countries (25 percent) and India (15 percent), as well as France, Turkey and China. "Iran's Oil and Gas Wealth," Joint Economic

Committee *Research Report* no. 109-31, March 2006, http://www.house.gov/jec/publications/109/rr109-31.pdf.

17. Energy Information Administration, U.S. Department of Energy, "Country Analysis Brief: Iran," January 2006, http://www.eia.doe.gov/emeu/cabs/Iran/Background.html; "'Iran's Refining Capacity to Increase to 900,000,'" iranmania.com, February 19, 2006, http://www.iranmania.com/News/ArticleView/Default.asp?ArchiveNews=Yes&NewsCode=40656&NewsKind=CurrentAffairs.

18. Study by Iran's Institute for International Energy Studies, as cited in Ali Nourizadeh, "Exploring Iran's Military Options," *Al-Sharq al-Awsat* (London), January 23, 2006, http://aawsat.com/english/news.asp?section=3&id=3528.

19. David J. Lynch, "Political, Tech Hurdles Muddle Iran Oil Industry," *USA Today*, September 13, 2006, http://www.washingtontimes.com/world/20060703-122150-7536r.htm.

20. Gareth Smyth, "Iran 'Will Need $5bn Subsidy' to Avoid Petrol Rationing," *Financial Times* (London), May 28, 2006, http://news.ft.com/cms/s/0627359c-ee77-11da-820a-0000779e2340, i rssPage=3f6a0854-c8f8-11d7-81c6-0820abe49a01.html.

21. "Iran Faces a Gasoline Time Bomb," *Petroleum Intelligence Weekly* 45, iss. 38 (2006), 4.

22. Ibid. This includes upgrades to nine existing refineries in the Islamic Republic and the construction of three new plants in the country's south.

23. Ibid.

24. Paul Klebnikov, "Millionaire Mullahs." *Forbes*, July 21, 2003, http://www.forbes.com/forbes/2003/0721/056 print.html.

25. See, for example, "Mr. R's Misconduct," Baztab (Tehran), October 16, 2006.

26. Robert D. Kaplan, "A Bazaari's World," *The Atlantic Monthly* 277, iss. 3 (1996), 28.

27. Wilfried Buchta, *Who Rules Iran? The Structure of Power in the Islamic Republic* (Washington, DC: Washington Institute for Near East Policy and Konrad Adenauer Stiftung, 2000), 75.

28. "Bonyad Controls $3 Billion, Says Rafiqdoust," *Iran Brief*, June 1, 1995; Klebnikov, "Millionaire Mullahs."

29. Ibid.; See also Kenneth Katzman, Statement before the Joint Economic Committee of the United States Congress, July 25, 2006, http://www.house.gov/jec/hearings/testimony/109/07-25-06 iran Katzman.pdf.

30. "NIOC Undertaking Host of Projects to Boost Oil Output," *Middle East Economic Survey* XLVIII, no. 19 (2005), as cited in A.F. Alhajji, "Will Iran's Nuclear Standoff Cause a World Energy Crisis? (Part 1 of 2)," *Middle East Economic Survey* XLIX, no. 13 (2006) http://www.mees.com/postedarticles/oped/v49n13-5OD01.htm.

31. Kenneth Katzman, *The Iran-Libya Sanctions Act (ILSA)* (Washington: Congressional Research Service, July 21, 2003), 2.

32. George A. Lopez and David Cortright, "Economic Sanctions in Contemporary Global Relations," in David Cortright and George A. Lopez, eds. *Economic Sanctions: Panacea or Peacebuilding in a Post-Cold War World?* (Boulder: Westview Press, 1995), 9.

33. Ahmadinejad Promises Single Digit Inflation Rate," IRNA (Tehran), August 29, 2006, http://www.irna.ir/en/news/view/line-18/0608291476185916.htm; Gary Thomas, "Government Spending Fueling Inflation," *Voice of America*, July 13, 2006, http://www.payvand.com/news/06/jul/1113.html.

34. Ibid.

35. See, for example, "UN Sanctions Should Weaken Support for Iran's Ahmadinejad, Expert Says," *Radio Free Europe/Radio Liberty Press Room*, March 3, 2006, http://www.rferl.org/releases/2006/03/388-030306.asp.

36. Figures derived from "Islamic Republic of Iran—Statistical Appendix," International Monetary Fund *Country Report* no. 04/307, September 2004, http://www.imf.org/external/pubs/ft/scr/2004/cr04307.pdf.

37. Ibid.

38. Ibidem; Wendy Cutler, Testimony before the Ways and Means Committee of the U.S. House of Representatives, September 28, 2005, http://waysandmeans.house.gov/hearings.asp?formmode=view&id=3793.

39. *Iran and Libya Sanctions Act of 1996*, Public Law 104-172, August 5, 1996, http://www.mipt.org/pdf/iranandlibyasanction104-172.pdf.

40. In its official response to the initial introduction of the Iran Freedom Support Act by Senator Rick Santorum (R-PA) to the Senate Foreign Relations Committee in June 2006, the Department of State declared that it opposed the measure on account of the fact that it would "create a rift between the U.S. and our closest international partners" and limit the Administration's "diplomatic flexibility." Assistant Secretary of State for Legislative Affairs Jeffrey T. Bergner, letter to Senate Foreign Relations Committee Chairman John Warner dated June 15, 2006 (author's collection).

41. "Iran Moves Assets to China, East Asia, worldtribune.com, January 23, 2006, http://www.worldtribune.com/worldtribune/06/front2453758.41875.html.

42. Meysam Salehian, "Central Bank vs. Government," *Rooz* (Tehran), May 10, 2006, http://roozonline.com/english/015477.shtml.

43. Christian Oliver, "Iran to Halt Gasoline Imports, Impose Rationing," Reuters, June 23, 2006; "Iran Calls Halt to Petrol Imports," BBC (London), June 23, 2006.

44. Alhajji, "Will Iran's Nuclear Standoff Cause a World Energy Crisis? (Part 1 of 2)."

ACTIVATING THE HUMAN RIGHTS DIMENSION

Sam Brownback

Although Iran's human rights record is every bit as disturbing as its support for international terrorism and its nuclear ambitions, policymakers rarely make human rights a top priority. All too often, they believe discussions of human rights and political reform should take place only after the resolution of any outstanding security issues.[1]

This constitutes a critical error. The nature of the regime in Tehran is intimately tied to its drive for nuclear weapons, its state sponsorship of terror and its often brutal treatment of its people. We should not be surprised that a regime that talks of wiping Israel off the map also denies its people freedom of expression. Nor should we be surprised that a regime that tortures its political opponents would employ terrorism as foreign policy. The issues of democracy and human rights should be as important to U.S. policy on Iran as discussions of terrorism or the nuclear issue. Indeed, the United States will find the best opportunity to enhance regional security and advance its interests lies in understanding the struggle of the Iranian people and embracing their drive for human rights and political reform.

Obviously, it is to the benefit of the people of Iran to be able to chart their own future without fear of reprisals from Tehran's theocrats. But those who minimize the importance of Tehran's human rights record miss two other reasons why it is essential to promote liberalization in Iran.

The first is that pro-democracy and human rights policies have strategic significance. Countries that respect human rights make better business partners. They are less likely to engage in destabilizing behavior.

They have more credibility in diplomatic negotiations. Promoting these policies can moderate the behavior of otherwise intransigent regimes.

The parallels with the Cold War are obvious. The Soviet Union sponsored terrorism on a global scale, and relied on its nuclear deterrent to ensure consolidation of its territorial expansion. Yet the inclusion of human rights in the Helsinki Final Act ultimately leveraged Moscow's brutal internal policies against the regime itself, in the process accelerating the fall of the Evil Empire.

The second reason emphasizing human rights is essential is that Iran's radical, theocratic government and dismal human rights record limits progress in other areas. As long as the Iranian regime represses its people, its claims of a peaceful nuclear program will ring hollow. Nor is Iran likely to end its terrorism-as-statecraft policy while it shields itself from domestic criticism. The character of the regime drives its behavior, and improving human rights is crucial to changing that character.

Of course, this will require more than mere cheerleading for human rights and democracy. Building a liberal political order in Iran and improving the lives of the Iranian people will require hard work into the foreseeable future. But the future begins now, and this chapter discusses policies that will leverage the significance of human rights and democracy for the benefit of the people of Iran and for the security of the United States.

BUILT ON FEAR

It sounds like something out of a George Orwell novel. In 1984, the worst horrors occurred inside Room 101, but "section 209" of the notorious Evin Prison—where Tehran sends some of the biggest perceived threats to the regime—is frighteningly real. A UN working group on arbitrary detention practices called section 209 a "prison within a prison" for the systematic, large-scale use of absolute solitary confinement, frequently for very long periods."[2]

Abdolfatah Soltani is lucky. He survived section 209. A human rights lawyer, Soltani endured seven months of detention in a section 209 cell measuring five square meters. He had no access to the outside world—no lawyer, no visits from his family and no newspapers or a radio. Though he was not physically tortured, other reports indicate section 209 detainees undergo daily, multiple interrogations, sleep deprivation, and terrible physical abuse.[3]

The existence of a Section 209 suggests a much larger problem. A regime that kills journalists for taking pictures and isolates lawyers who call for human rights improvements will justify any action to ensure its hold on power. Evin Prison, then, is a tangible symbol of the regime's domination of Iranian society. Various assessments of Iran's human rights record paint a unanimously bleak picture. The State Department's most recent human rights report noted that "government's poor human rights record worsened [in 2005], and it continued to commit numerous, serious abuses."[4] Human Rights Watch concluded that respect for human rights in 2005 "deteriorated considerably."[5] Amnesty International noted that in 2005 hundreds of political prisoners were arrested, journalists and human rights defenders faced arbitrary detention, and torture remained common.[6] Freedom House rates each country in the world between 1 (highest degree of freedom) and 7 (lowest degree of freedom). Iran received a 6 in the latest survey.[7]

Iran's human rights problems date to the founding of the Islamic Republic of Iran. The radical Islamic theology promoted by the Ayatollah Khomeini provided the foundation upon which successor governments have based their legitimacy. Today, Iran continues to fuse mosque and state into a system where dissent—be it political, social or religious—represents a threat to the government's self-appointed legitimacy.

The regime's radicalism imposes unrealistic and unnatural constraints on Iranian society, from the standard authoritarian restrictions on free speech to official bans on Iranian women wearing loose headscarves or tight jackets.[8] Dissent, under these conditions, is a given. And ever-present dissent sparks ever-present repression. The inner workings of this vicious cycle can be observed in the structure of the Iranian government, the targets of government repression and the nature and intensity of that repression.

Iran's government itself is built for repression. Despite occasional elections, it is no democracy. Iran is a true theocracy, where the religious elites hold ultimate authority. They are led by a supreme leader who holds limitless veto power; appoints other key government and military leaders and confirms the election of the president. Unelected and subject to almost no oversight, the supreme leader is both the most powerful political actor in Iran and personally responsible for carrying forward Khomeini's Islamic Revolution.

The religious elites at the heart of the Iranian government have created quasi-official bodies to ensure their will is exercised. According to Human Rights Watch, many of Iran's human rights violations in

2005 came at the hands of "parallel institutions" including "paramilitary groups and plainclothes intelligence agents [that] violently attack peaceful protesters, and intelligence services [that] run illegal secret prisons and interrogation centers."[9]

In recent years, some analysts held out hope that "reformers" within Iran's government could moderate the regime's behavior. Indeed, many Iranians believed that the 1997 election of Mohammad Khatami heralded a new era of reform in Iran. Khatami, however, proved unable to meet the expectations of the people—a reality hammered home by the deterioration of human rights on his watch. Momentum for reform stalled. By the time of his departure from the political scene in 2005, it had become clear that "reformers" like Khatami were either powerless, or insincere.

Thanks in no small measure to the religious elites' management of Iranian elections—allowing only ideologically acceptable candidates to run for office—conservative hardliners have made significant gains in recent years, culminating with the 2005 election of President Mahmoud Ahmadinejad. These gains only serve to confirm that the very structure of the Iranian system limits the scope of reform that can occur from within the government.

This structure has manifested itself in brutal ways. The regime focuses on punishing those behaviors that appear to cross the regime's extremist Islamic *raison d'etre*—even if those engaged in such activities do not intend to be politically subversive. Since taking office, Ahmadinejad has launched a concerted campaign of domestic repression, including new restrictions on radio, television, and film content, a ban on the publication of virtually all books, and an expansion of the activities of the regime's "morality police."[10] President Ahmadinejad also has moved to limit freedom of expression in higher education. His concerns about secularism in Iranian universities led him, on September 5, 2006, to call for a purge of all liberal and secular faculty members.[11]

And as one would guess, religious minorities face particular oppression. Since 1999, the Secretary of State has designated Iran as a country of particular concern under the International Religious Freedom Act, and the State Department's latest religious freedom report noted that 2005 saw "a further deterioration of the extremely poor status of respect for religious freedom."[12] Iran's Baha'is, Jews, Christians, Mandaeans, and Zoroastrians face discrimination, imprisonment, harassment, and intimidation because they exist outside the dominant religious order.

The regime guarantees swift and severe penalties for those that resist its constraints on society. The declining human rights situation within the country is marked by torture, stonings, amputations, floggings, and beheadings as routine methods of punishment. The reliance on such brutality underscores the regime's desire to deter those who would act against the regime in the future.

The Iranian Republic's very existence, in short, depends on repression. The regime is structured to facilitate simple and efficient repression, targeting in particular those activities that threaten Iran's theocratic precepts and administering horrible punishments that reinforce the seriousness with which it takes the threat of political, social and religious non-conformity.

Leveraging human rights

There are those who believe that trying to improve the lives of the Iranian people may impede our efforts to dismantle the regime's nuclear program or end Iranian support for terrorism. Ultimately, however, the reverse will prove true: focusing on human rights and democratic reforms is the best way to moderate Iran's foreign policy. Iran's intransigence on the nuclear issue points to the difficulty associated with changing the regime's domestic policies. Yet the United States and its allies can facilitate changes inside Iran in a number of ways.

A regional framework for Iranian human rights

In 1975, the United States and its western allies reached agreement with the Soviet Union on the Helsinki Final Act. That document offered certain political and security guarantees to the Soviet Union, but also required that members of the newly created Conference on Security and Cooperation in Europe (CSCE)—including the USSR—would "recognize the universal significance of human rights and fundamental freedoms, respect for which is an essential factor for the peace, justice and well-being necessary to ensure the development of friendly relations and co-operation among themselves as among all States."[13] With its signature, the Soviet Union legitimated international criticism of its human rights record, and emboldened dissidents inside the USSR to hold Moscow accountable for the treatment of its own people. We should pay close attention to this lesson from recent history.

The Helsinki process is successful because states make political commitments on a wide range of issues. Because the penalty for not keeping a commitment is political, countries within the Helsinki framework have an incentive to keep their word in order to maintain credibility both with other states and with their own people. Because Helsinki covers a wide range of issues from security and economics to human rights, members must take all commitments seriously. A country attempting to downplay its human rights commitments risks criticism from the same countries from which it expects to receive security assurances and economic benefits.

Could this process be applied to Iran? To be sure, there are differences between present-day Iran and the Soviet Union in 1975, and Iran's participation in such an arrangement remains a distant prospect. But as one-time Soviet dissident Natan Sharansky has put it, "the free world does not need to wait for dictatorial regimes to consent to reform... if we condition reform [on] the agreement [of] non-democratic leaders, it may never come. We must be prepared to move forward on the policy of linkage, despite their objections."[14]

To begin, Helsinki participants should require Iran to meet the same standards on human rights to which they have committed themselves. Under Helsinki's human dimension, countries make commitments in several areas, including scientific cooperation, the movement of people, freedom of information and educational exchanges. These countries should begin to make Iran adhere to some of these standards as a prerequisite to relations in other areas.

Make no mistake, convincing Helsinki countries to begin applying these standards would be difficult, especially since many countries would probably be forced to put their economic relationships with Iran at risk. But there are a few reasons for optimism. First, for all of the policy differences between the United States and its trans-Atlantic partners, both sides of the Atlantic affirm the importance of universal human rights. If the United States is willing to link the nuclear issue to human rights, European nations may be more amenable to enforcing human rights standards in Iran. Second, as a Freedom House representative told a Helsinki Commission hearing on Iran in 2005, there is a growing belief, particularly in central and Eastern Europe, that more should be done to address democratic challenges in Iran and other areas beyond Europe's borders.[15] The same locations that experienced Soviet tyranny first-hand apparently have sharp instincts for addressing present-day tyrannical regimes.

Third, members of the Helsinki process face a shared security threat from Iran's nuclear program and terrorism. They also maintain a commitment to the principle that human rights are issues of universal concern. This common ground allows a country to call for improved human rights in Iran not on the basis of unilateral or selfish interests, but in the context of time-honored multilateral agreements that already exist among the 55 Helsinki participants.

The ultimate goal of a Helsinki-style process for Iran should be the development of an international consensus on Iran policy—a broad-based agreement that Iran should be held accountable for its actions in the security, economic and human rights spheres. Today, Iran has no reason to listen to the world's concerns, but the broad application of internationally-approved standards of conduct might convince Iran to engage in serious negotiations instead of isolating itself from the rest of the world. As the Soviet example suggests, if and when that occurs, it will be a major victory for the Iranian people and a turning point for U.S. Iran policy.

Empowering dissident leaders

A Helsinki process for Iran is only the beginning, however. Even as human rights issues have been marginalized during Iran's push for a nuclear weapons capability, the Iranian people's frustration with conditions in their country has spawned a broad-based movement—including all sectors of Iranian society, from youth and students to women, military personnel and religious figures—desiring political change.

This movement, however, lacks consistent leadership, particularly because Tehran acts violently against those who rise to prominence by opposing the regime. Akbar Mohammadi, for example, received a fifteen year sentence in Evin Prison for his role in the July 1999 student protests. When he was released from prison to address medical concerns, he wrote a prison memoir that landed him back at Evin, where he later died. To add insult to injury, his parents, who were visiting their daughter in Turkey when he died, returned to Tehran only to be detained and escorted to their home in Amol without seeing their son's body.[16] The Iranian opposition movement will not achieve the changes it desires, or coalesce around a coherent reform platform, until it can identify strong leaders who have time to organize before being incarcerated.

The outside world can help here. First, the United States and other nations should pay more attention to particular cases of human rights abuse in Iran. Such attention amounts to more than an excuse to score rhetorical points against Tehran. International attention may help anoint some dissidents as leaders in the human rights and democracy movement. Other Iranians also might be inspired to join the cause of reform based on reports of the bravery of regime opponents.

In addition, an international spotlight can limit or perhaps eliminate regime retaliation. The case of Roya Toloui is instructive. Toloui, an Iranian Kurdish women's rights activist, was falsely accused of leading protests against the regime, arrested and thrown into an intelligence prison. She underwent three months of abuse before confessing to crimes she did not commit out of fear for the lives of her children. She thought she would die in jail, but obtained her release after international human rights groups pressured Tehran to let her go. She later left Iran and moved to the United States, where she continues to call for improved human rights in Iran.[17]

Toloui was lucky. Others never get a second chance to speak out against the regime. Consequently, the identification of dissidents before they are imprisoned is crucial, especially if they are to call for reform from inside Iran.

Second, private and non-governmental organizations should receive greater support for the many ways in which they can promote change in Iran. They can spotlight the causes of individual reformers, receive and disseminate the news and information reformers provide that is otherwise unavailable from the state-controlled media, transmit news and perspectives from the outside world to reformers inside Iran, and contribute to the development of a strong Iranian civil society. The future of reform in Iran depends in no small part on two-way communication between Iranian reformers who best understand the internal dynamics of their country and outside organizations positioned to provide assistance where necessary.

In recent years, Congress has appropriated relatively small sums to support democracy in Iran, and in the fall of 2006 it authorized the President to give financial and political assistance to organizations that reject terrorism and support peaceful democratic changes in Iran.[18] Now that Congress has specified the conditions under which democracy funds can be distributed, it should increase its appropriations substantially. Congress should not force the State Department to squeeze money out of existing grant programs in order to fund entities of such significance. Instead, future budgets should make support for democracy in Iran an explicit priority.

Another way for dissidents to report on the conditions inside Iran—and their opinions on those conditions—is through the Internet, especially through Internet weblogs, or blogs. Iran's population is young, computer literate and eager to express its criticism of the regime, even on topics as politically sensitive as President Ahmadinejad's drive for a nuclear capability. The presence of as many as 100,000 active Iranian blogs allows for first-hand accounts of events never reported in the state-controlled press, as well as the widespread dissemination of individual opinions. Blogs can also serve as mechanisms to organize opposition activities, and as channels through which the reality of life inside Iran can be transmitted to the rest of the world. The Iranian government's minimally successful efforts to eliminate Iranian blogs reinforce the potential impact of the Iranian blogosphere.[19] Policymakers, therefore, should be attentive to Internet freedoms in Iran and work to ensure the virtual world remains open and accessible to Iranians seeking reforms.

Broadcasting

The United States broke off diplomatic relations with Iran after the 1979 hostage crisis. Economic relations are nearly non-existent thanks to a variety of measures, most notably the Iran-Libya Sanctions Act. By design, interactions between the U.S. and Iran are sporadic and indirect. Only one facet of U.S. policy involves consistent and direct interaction with Iran: foreign broadcasting.

The utility of these broadcasts should not be underestimated. During the Cold War, the U.S. funded broadcasts around the world as a way to check the spread of communism and spark reforms behind the Iron Curtain. Radio Free Europe and the Voice of America provided information lifelines for dissidents and reformers who in turn played a crucial role in hastening communism's defeat.

As in the Cold War, U.S. broadcasts provide an opportunity to by pass the regime and speak directly to the Iranian people. Another chapter in this volume discusses how to fashion appropriate messages for transmission through the U.S. foreign broadcasting apparatus. But to ensure that such a message, once articulated, leaves Washington and enters Iran, Congress will have to reconsider some of the constraints placed on foreign broadcasts.

In order to ensure U.S. broadcasts did not lapse into the kind of propaganda that emanated from the Soviet Union, broadcasters during the Cold War were kept separate from foreign policy decision makers at the State Department. U.S. broadcasts were free to provide unbiased news, even if events adjusted U.S. foreign policy priorities from one day to the next. Even after post-Cold War reforms to U.S. public diplomacy, the Broadcasting Board of Governors (BBG) stands between policy makers and the content transmitted through U.S. broadcasts.

Iran presents a new challenge, however. Iranians with the ability to view Voice of America Persian Service television, for example, are also likely to have access to CNN or the BBC. Since they know VOA broadcasts emanate from the U.S., they expect to hear a U.S. perspective—not just the reports they could get from the world's private global news giants. In Iran, VOA must set a goal not to outperform CNN, but to ensure the U.S. perspective is available among a wide range of choices.

Today, VOA often falls short of this goal. Its charter calls for the VOA to be "accurate, objective, and comprehensive" and to "present the policies of the United States clearly and effectively..."[20] But VOA often emphasizes the former requirement at the expense of the latter. The Persian Service is so concerned with objectivity that it gives undue deference to the positions of the Iranian government. A story on human rights abuses in Iran, for example, might be "balanced" by Iranian government criticisms of human rights in the United States. Such an approach turns objectivity on its head: Iranian officials should be allowed to explain the reasons why an alleged human rights violation occurred, but they deserve no U.S.-sponsored airtime to criticize the United States.

Worse, the Persian Service and its counterpart, Radio Farda, often rely on official Islamic Republic sources to fill out news broadcasts. Nothing could be more demoralizing for prospective human rights advocates and democratic reformers than hearing messages from the regime on broadcasts they know are funded by the United States.

Of course, the Persian Service and Radio Farda should not be converted to U.S. propaganda outlets, but closer Congressional oversight is in order. Having provided more than $30 million in supplemental appropriations in 2006 to expand broadcasting into Iran, Congress must ensure taxpayer funds are spent wisely. Congress should therefore review carefully the content of U.S. broadcasts—something that will require the BBG to provide English translations of Persian language broadcasts and make regular reports about programming decisions. More importantly, however, decisions about programming should be made through a collaboration of policymakers at the State Department and the broadcasting experts at the BBG. Such an effort could keep the possibility of actual bias in U.S. broadcasts to a minimum while ensuring that our most important interaction with the Iranian people offers a clear explanation of how the U.S. supports freedom and democracy for the people of Iran.

Finally, the United States should work closely with Iranian expatriates who send their own broadcasts into Iran. While the programming and quality of these private broadcasts varies greatly, such efforts are unlikely to inadvertently promote the views of the Iranian government. And as with the blogosphere, the regime's occasional responses to these broadcasts point to their effectiveness.[21] When Congress authorized support for pro-democracy groups, it specified that private broadcasters are eligible to receive government funds. But again, until substantial funds flow to these broadcasters this will remain an unfulfilled promise.

The bottom line is that Tehran understands the power of foreign broadcasts to expose the abuses of the regime, and to give Iranians access to unfiltered information from and about the outside world. Both official and private broadcasts therefore represent an invaluable tool for U.S. policymakers to turn concern for human rights and reform into calls for action.

A special envoy for Iranian human rights

Above, I have discussed a series of steps to emphasize the importance of human rights and harness the power of the Iranian people to change the character of the regime that oppresses them. To implement and coordinate these policies, I have proposed that the United States establish a "special envoy" within the State Department with a specific focus on human rights and democracy in Iran.

A special envoy would be beneficial for several reasons. First, a special envoy could help integrate pro-human rights and democracy policies into the day-to-day activities of the various offices that formulate Iran policy at the State Department and elsewhere (e.g., the Bureau of Near Eastern Affairs, the Bureau of Nonproliferation, the BBG, USAID and various offices in the Department of Defense and the National Security Council). It is unreasonable to ask so many parts of the bureaucracy to execute the wide variety of policies discussed above and maintain their cohesion and effectiveness. A special envoy could help ensure U.S. efforts to promote human rights and democracy do not fragment along bureaucratic fault lines.

Second, the special envoy would develop a close relationship with private and non-governmental organizations. I have already discussed several ways in which individuals and groups outside the U.S. government can play a key role in inducing Iranian reforms, and the special envoy could help harness the energy and passion of these groups.

Third, just as policy coordination inside the U.S. government is crucial, mobilizing international efforts to emphasize Iranian freedom and human rights is essential to the reform effort. The special envoy would be vital to persuading other countries of the importance of human rights and spearheading the establishment of the regional framework on human rights in Iran.

But the final benefit of a special envoy is perhaps the most important: by working within the U.S. government, alongside like-minded foreign governments and with private and non-governmental groups, the special envoy will be able to ensure that human rights and democracy become an essential part of the foundation of U.S. policy toward Iran. This would represent an enormous boost to the reformers now struggling inside the Islamic Republic.

And their success can be our success. Not only do we desire a better life for the Iranian people, we hope for a democratic government that behaves as a modern, responsible state whose word in international negotiations can be trusted. If, as the saying goes, a man can be judged by the company he keeps, a government ought to be judged by the way it treats its people. If Iran's human rights record improves, and if its government more closely reflects the will of the people, a more stable Middle East—and by extension, better security for the United States—will follow.

Endnotes

1. For example, the U.S. Senate refused to act on either the Iran Democracy Act I introduced in 2003 or the Iran amendment Senator Rick Santorum offered to the 2006 Defense authorization bill (Congress ultimately passed a scaled-down version of that amendment). While many lawmakers expressed support for these measures in principle, they—often under pressure from the State Department—deemed ongoing nuclear negotiations too delicate to disrupt with conversations about democracy and human rights.

2. United Nations Commission on Human Rights, Working Group on Arbitrary Detention, "Visit to the Islamic Republic of Iran, 15-27 February 2003," June 27, 2003, 15.

3. Golnaz Esfandiari, "Iran: Rights Groups Want Investigation Of Evin Prison," *Radio Free Europe/Radio Liberty*, October 26, 2006, http://rfe.rferl.org/featuresarticle/2006/10/2ae58926-1179-4668-ae1d-b61924d5437d.html?rapage=1.

4. U.S. Department of State, Bureau of Democracy, Human Rights and Labor, "Country Reports on Human Rights Practices: Iran," March 8, 2006, http://www.state.gov/g/drl/rls/hrrpt/2005/61688.htm.

5. Human Rights Watch, "Human Rights Overview: Iran," January 18, 2006, http://hrw.org/english/docs/2006/01/18/iran12214.htm.

6. "Iran," *Amnesty International Annual Country Report 2006*, n.d, http://www.amnestyusa.org/countries/iran/document.do?id=ar&yr=2006.

7. "Iran" *Freedom House Country Report 2006*, n.d., http://www.freedomhouse.org/template.cfm?page=22&year=2006&country=6982.

8. Robert Tait, "Police in Tehran Ordered to Arrest Women in 'un-Islamic' Dress," *Guardian* (London), April 20, 2006, http://www.guardian.co.uk/international/story/0,,1757002,00.html.

9. Human Rights Watch, "Human Rights Overview: Iran."

10. See Ilan Berman, "Understanding Ahmadinejad," American Foreign Policy Council *Iran Strategy Brief* no. 1, June 2006, http://www.afpc.org/IFI/UnderstandingAhmadinejad.pdf.

11. Ladane Nasseri, "Iran's Ahmadinejad Urges Purge of Secular Academics," Bloomberg, September 5, 2006, http://www.bloomberg.com/apps/news?pid=20601100&sid=aVaNIdJJvcNU&refer=germany.

12. U.S. Department of State, Bureau of Democracy, Human Rights and Labor, "International Religious Freedom Report 2006: Iran," September 15, 2006, http://www.state.gov/g/drl/rls/irf/2006/71421.htm.

13. *Conference on Security and Co-operation in Europe Final Act*, Helsinki, Norway, August 1, 1975, 6, http://www.osce.org/documents/mcs/1975/08/4044_en.pdf.

14. Natan Sharansky, Testimony before the U.S. Commission on Security and Cooperation in Europe, June 15, 2004, http://www.csce.gov/index.cfm?Fuseaction=ContentRecords.ViewDetail&ContentRecord_id=280&Region_id=0&Issue_id=0&ContentType=H,B&ContentRecordType=H&CFID=24114908&CFTOKEN=31740397.

15. Tom Melia, Testimony before the U.S. Commission on Security and Cooperation in Europe, June 9, 2005, http://www.csce.gov/index.cfm?Fuseaction=ContentRecords.ViewTranscript&ContentRecord_id=351&ContentType=H,B&ContentRecordType=H&CFID=24114908&CFTOKEN=31740397.

16. "Iran: Akbar Mohammadi's Death in Custody Signals Need for Justice Reform," Amnesty International Press Release, August 1, 2006, http://www.amnestyusa.org/news/document.do?id=ENGMDE130862006.

17. Golnaz Estaandiari and Farin Assemi, "Iran: Kurdish Women's Rights Activist Claims She Was Tortured in Prison," *Radio Free Europe/Radio Liberty*, February 1, 2006; http://www.rferl.org/featuresarticle/2006/02/018e8424-74c5-4f77-a00b-444cdc86061c.html.

18. *Iran Freedom Support Act*, Public Law 109-293, September 30, 2006, http://frwebgate.access.gpo.gov/cgi-bin/getdoc.cgi?dbname=109_cong_public_laws&docid=f:publ293.109.pdf.

19. Daniel W. Drezner and Henry Farrell, "Web of Influence," *Foreign Policy*, November/December 2004, http://www.foreignpolicy.com/story/cms.php?story_id=2707&page=0; Ben Macintyre, "Mullahs Versus the Bloggers," *Times of London*, December 23, 2005, http://www.timesonline.co.uk/article/0,,1068-1957461,00.html; "Iranian Blogs Debate Nuclear Row," BBC, January 31, 2006, http://news.bbc.co.uk/2/hi/middle_east/4650154.stm.

20. Excerpts from the VOA Charter, http://www.voanews.com/english/about/VOACharter.cfm.

21. Gordon Smith, "TV Stations Add Voice to Debate in Iran," *San Diego Union Tribune*, July 30, 2006, http://www.signonsandiego.com/uniontrib/20060730/news_ln30irantv.html.

THE LIMITS OF ALLIED ACTION

Stephen J. Blank

The diplomatic struggle to compel Iran to renounce its nuclear ambitions is approaching a climax. The Bush administration's May 30, 2006 decision to engage Iran directly should it give up uranium enrichment has presented the Islamic Republic with a stark choice: pursue nuclearization and risk sanctions, or opt for the benefits it claims to desire through direct talks with Washington.[1] And Iran appears to have made its choice; as of this writing, the Iranian regime is forging ahead with its nuclear program, confident in the belief that it runs no serious risks by so doing, and that its two principal strategic partners, Russia and China, will protect it from any serious international repercussions.[2] In short, the international negotiating process over Iran's nuclear program shows every sign of breaking down, and probably sooner rather than later. If Iran's belief that it can proceed with impunity is correct, such a breakdown will confront the United States and its international partners with the possibility of having to use force to end Iran's nuclear effort.

This is not a farfetched possibility. Russia, a permanent member of the United Nations Security Council, has repeatedly refused to contemplate the threat of international sanctions, despite Iran's failure to abide by UN demands.[3] China has similarly assumed an unconstructive stance, insisting on "diplomacy" as the sole means of resolving the Iranian nuclear impasse.[4] Should the UN be blocked from action by a Russian or Chinese veto, and if the current six-party negotiating process likewise bogs down, the likelihood of the use of force will increase dramatically.

Goodbye to Europe

It cannot be said that America's European allies do not understand the strategic implications of a nuclear-armed Iran. As former French Foreign Minister Herve de Charette has declared, "When violence returns to the Middle East, sooner or later it will show up in Paris."[5] The question is whether, should the option of using force arise, Washington can confidently rely on support from its strategic partners in Europe.

By way of further definition, it is clear that any such operation will need to be precipitated by a clear and egregious violation of the Nuclear Nonproliferation Treaty (NPT), or by an offensive, and probably no less forceful, action on the part of Iran. It is, or should be, absolutely clear that NATO as an alliance will not (and probably could not) undertake an offensive and unprovoked operation—i.e., either a preemptive strike or a preventive war—against Iran, without extensive diplomatic and political urging by Washington and exceptionally clumsy and offensive behavior from Tehran. European public opinion will not easily support any attack against Iran that is not authorized by the UN—even if NATO were to endorse it—unless Iran attacked first.[6] And, while there can be no doubt that NATO as an organization (and the British and American governments individually) is seriously discussing contingencies for military action,[7] there is a profound ambivalence in the European Union about using force to achieve security in the Middle East.

The factors making any future NATO operation against Iran so difficult to imagine are numerous, ranging from the political to the operational.

First, as the experience of the Kosovo conflict has clearly shown, we can rule out preemptive or preventive operations unless there truly is a demonstrably "clear and present danger" of threatening Iranian action. Second, since any member of NATO can veto an operation, the basis and justification for launching one must be carefully prepared and no less carefully delineated, so as to gain universal support. Therefore, it is highly unlikely that a genuine consensus could be built for a U.S.-led preemptive strike, especially after the experience of Iraq.

Third, it is not clear that the Treaty of Washington provides an undisputed legal basis for a preventive war or preemptive operation, especially since so many Europeans insist that only the UN can approve military operations other than those strictly for self-defense. Consequently, we could well end up with a situation like the one that prevailed in 2003, when key members refused to invoke Article V of the Treaty to defend Turkey in the event of an Iraqi attack.

Fourth, the political and military objectives of any such operation, as well the procedures for making tactical readjustments, will need to be fully worked out among participating members ahead of time. These considerations obviously rule out *post facto* NATO support for a unilateral preventive strike by Washington. The difficulties we have seen in convincing NATO members to send forces to Afghanistan, and of enlarging their remit and rules of engagement in that theater, where there is no question of the operation's legitimacy, further underscores the problems involved in gaining NATO's timely assent for any preventive strike—or for actually getting sufficient usable forces and sufficiently flexible rules of engagement for them.

Fifth, even before the invasion of Iraq in 2003, NATO consistently found it difficult to consider so-called "out of area" operations in the Middle East.[8] Even if one assumes that the Alliance has steadily widened its sphere of action in the region over the past half-decade, the scale of those activities remains relatively small, and has emerged only after prolonged debate and much reluctance.[9] NATO will also need partners if it is to act effectively in the Middle East, and it is doubtful that many regional governments will support preemption or preventive war against Iran in that context.[10] Indeed, attacking Iran has the potential to reignite the bitter divisions of 2003, and could shatter an Alliance that many observers believe is already in a highly precarious state.[11]

We should remember here that unilateral European or American operations in the Middle East have almost always stimulated divisions among the allies. Iraq may constitute the greatest crisis in NATO since the 1956 Suez crisis, but it has not been the only one. Traditionally, the Alliance has had difficulty accepting instances in which its members have launched preventative wars in the Middle East on their own. And even if one takes into account the efforts that have been made to repair Transatlantic harmony over Iran, the underlying grounds for European skepticism of, if not downright opposition to, U.S. objectives and threat assessments appear to remain fundamentally intact.[12]

American officials are cognizant of these realities. Already in 2004, U.S. observers were conceding that, "[o]ther than Israel, few if any U.S. allies would be willing or able to carry out such an operation."[13] More recently, a study compiled by the EU's Institute for Security Studies confirmed that European opposition to a unilateral American operation against Iran would be wide and deep: "Needless to say, as seen from a European point of view, US military action against Iran would be just as unwelcome an outcome as an Iranian nuclear weapons capability."[14]

Obviously, this reluctance to contemplate the possibility that force might be the only feasible option undermines the credibility of any diplomatic representations that the EU-3 might make to Iran. But Europeans do not appear to be deterred; indeed, Nicole Gnesotto, the Director of the EU's Institute for Security Studies, interpreted the State Department's May 30, 2006 offer of direct negotiations with Iran as a great victory for Europe in approaches to the crisis.[15] This sentiment not only underscores the ongoing mutual suspicions festering at the heart of the Atlantic Alliance, but also the fact that a European foreign and security policy capable of unified action is still more a wish than a reality. It is not without merit that Iranians believe the West to be a paper tiger.

Another issue is present as well. Nearly four years after the initiation of hostilities, the specter of Iraq continues to loom large in the calculus of America's allies across the Atlantic. The tensions surrounding Operation Iraqi Freedom are not gone, nor are they forgotten. They continue to hamstring effective cooperation among the NATO allies in the Middle East. Most fundamentally, they reflect a deep disjunction among the U.S. and its allies of the way to fight both terrorism and proliferation.[16] Moreover, this gap in threat perceptions, not to mention lingering European distrust of Washington, remains very much in effect today, even though the EU's formative strategic document identifies proliferation as the greatest potential threat to European security.[17] As such, there is limited political support in Europe for an operation against Iran—an attitude that is quite likely to considerably reduce allied burdensharing in the event of a military crisis.[18]

Indeed, despite the fact that both sides of the Atlantic have identified common threats to their security, Europe views the use of force with the greatest reluctance, even beyond calling it a last resort. Thus, perhaps the most fundamental reason that European military support for an attack against Iran is unlikely is that a forceful riposte goes against the very grain of the EU's entire international security ethos. That ethos is embodied in the 2003 European Security Strategy (ESS) authored by EU foreign policy czar Javier Solana. Although it postulates that proliferation and terrorism are the greatest threats facing Europe, the ESS focuses primarily on political, rather than military, means in order to overcome them.[19]

This should provide a foretaste of Europe's preferred responses to the Iranian threat. As analyst James Sperling has noted, under the formulation embraced by the ESS, a range of threats—from transnational terrorism to the proliferation of weapons of mass destruction to regional conflicts—"do not necessarily call for large-scale investments in power projection capabilities."[20] On the contrary, the ESS "underscores that 'none of these threats is purely military; nor can any be tackled by purely military means' and claims that the EU is 'particularly well-equipped' to meet the diplomatic, civil, and economic requirements attending the new threats."[21]

As the foregoing suggests, the EU's core strategic objectives comprise conflict and threat prevention, building stability in its neighborhood, and the reinforcement of multilateralism embodied by "well-functioning international institutions... and a rule-based international order."[22] While these priorities are not anti-American *per se*, their emphasis on the political and economic hardly augurs well for Europe's readiness to contemplate forcing Iran to desist from nuclearization.

Yet even if the requisite political will to strike Iran was visible, the operational structure of European forces strongly militates against NATO or the EU being able to provide the necessary forces for such a combat operation. Simply put, while U.S. forces are galloping forward in their efforts to augment capabilities for high-tech joint interoperability and power projection, their European counterparts (with few exceptions) are undeployable for anything other than so-called "stability operations" or non-combat missions.[23]

All this will serve to make practical cooperation among militaries very difficult. Certainly, EU forces alone could not undertake a military operation to denuclearize Iran, and possibly even fight a war with it—although they might be well-situated to assume a future post-conflict stability role. Moreover, even an EU or NATO stability operations force, if carried out in the foreseeable future, likely would have to rely greatly upon U.S. electronic air and air defense assets, communications, command, control, and intelligence, and airlift to overcome potential shortfalls in capability. As Dutch analyst Rob de Wijk observed in 2004, "[m]ost European forces are still in-place forces. This explains why only 10 to 15 percent of NATO's forces are deployable."[24] While matters may have improved somewhat, it is still the case that budgetary outlays are not keeping pace with force requirements in Europe.[25]

The desirability of such an operation is not the issue; if the six-party negotiators or the EU-3 and Washington concur on the need for a sustained military operation, then capabilities will become very important. And, if the foregoing is any indication, Washington would very likely find itself largely on its own.

Captive Nations

In the event of a military confrontation with Iran, air power will be indispensable. Under practically every conceivable military scenario, air strikes will be necessary to supress Iranian air defenses, or to cripple or terminate Iran's nuclear program. But where would such firepower be based?

The logical candidates are the former Soviet Republics of the Caucasus and Central Asia. These countries have assumed major strategic importance for the United States since the start of the War on Terror, providing crucial and ongoing assistance in both major theaters of military operations: Afghanistan and Iraq. But action against Iran would go beyond simply hosting air bases from which strikes against Iran could be launched. It would include overflight rights, refueling rights, logistical support, medical evacuation and airlift, among other possible non-combat functions.

Unfortunately, at least at present, using bases in those states for such purposes is almost inconceivable. America's extensive post-9/11 regional foothold has steadily eroded over the past several years, and U.S. efforts to maintain its strategic influence there have so far been unsuccessful.[26] Thus, even though Washington is certainly concerned about Iranian influence in the "post-Soviet space,"[27] its ability to counteract such influence today is limited, for a number of reasons.

First, any government in the Commonwealth of Independent States (CIS) that permits a new U.S. base in its territory would immediately be faced with real threats from Russia. Both Russia and China view any American presence in Central Asia as inimical to their vital interests, and as a long-term military, ideological and political challenge that must be countered. Along those lines, senior officials such as Russian Defense Minister Sergei Ivanov and Foreign Minister Sergei Lavrov have made clear that Moscow now demands a veto power over other CIS members' defense ties to the West,[28] and have warned of dire economic and political consequences if the Kremlin finds "disloyal" governments within the CIS.[29] Indeed, since 2002, Russia and China have sought to pressure the U.S. to leave its existing bases in Central Asia, and to prevent the extension of U.S. basing rights in the Caucasus (namely Azerbaijan and Georgia).[30] Therefore, any U.S. initiative to the contrary can be expected to trigger serious pressure from Moscow (if not Beijing)—pressure that would probably suffice by itself in deterring those states from responding positively.

Second, there are limits to the current cooperative arrangements established by the United States with regional nations. The agreement regulating the use of the U.S. base at Manas in Kyrgyzstan, for example, does not allow its use for combat operation unrelated to the war in Afghanistan. This certainly is an important legal-political argument in its own right, but it can also provide a strong political shield behind which to conceal the reality that it is not only Russian pressure that these states are worried about. Indeed, with both Russia and Iran as neighbors, the countries of both regions are well aware of the risks of appearing to lean too overtly to the American side.[31] In May 2005, on the heels of Secretary of Defense Donald Rumsfeld's very public visit to Baku, the Azeri government inked a non-aggression pact with Iran barring third countries from establishing bases in their countries to strike at the other side—making its opposition to a military strike emanating from its country crystal clear.[32] Other states have confined themselves to anodyne or neutral statements confirming Iran's rights under the NPT, but clearly hoping that it does not go nuclear and threaten them.[33] In fact, Kazakhstan, perhaps trying to show its regional leadership in Central Asia, has recently attempted to take on the role of mediator between Iran and the EU.[34]

This wavering is understandable. After all, even a non-nuclear Iran poses a serious threat to its neighbors on the other shore of the Caspian on at least three fronts.

The first is military. Iranian officials have made clear that they want Washington to regard their country as a "big regional power," and this vision clearly spans the Caspian region.[35] This desire has led Iran to assume an increasingly aggressive military posture in the Caspian in recent years. Back in 2001, Iran forced a temporary freeze on energy development in the region when it attacked Azeri oil platforms.[36] Since then, it has attempted repeatedly to do the same with Kazakhstan's energy operations.[37] Iran is also expanding its military capabilities in the region. As a recent study by the Center for Strategic & International Studies has noted, Iran's ability to conduct asymmetric warfare in the Caspian Sea and its littoral—a capability that could involve both its regular armed forces and the regime's elite Islamic Revolutionary Guards Corps, or Pasdaran—is expanding. As a result, Iran's naval and other forces are acquiring greater ability to conduct limited or unconventional warfare, threaten traffic through the Gulf (or the Caspian) and intimidate Iran's regional neighbors.[38]

But if those capabilities do not suffice to deter regional states, then the possibility of Iranian-backed insurgency or terror operations in Central Asia and the Caucasus probably will. Such activities would not be difficult for Iran to coordinate, given its deep support for international terrorist entities such as Hezbollah, Hamas, the Palestinian Islamic Jihad, and even al-Qaeda. Certainly, there have been persistent reports of Iranian underground activities, particularly in Tajikistan and Azerbaijan.[39] And there is considerable evidence that Iran is building up networks or relationships among Transcaucasian, Central Asian and Afghan insurgents and terrorists—ties that could be activated in the future to threaten those governments or American interests or bases in the region.[40] In 2002, the U.S. Central Command (USCENTCOM) uncovered intelligence showing that elements of the Pasdaran were secretly providing training and logistic support to the al-Qaeda affiliated Islamic Movement of Uzbekistan.[41] Iran has also been tied to support for radical religious and separatist movements in Azerbaijan, and in 2005 London's *Sunday Telegraph* reported that the Pasdaran had begun "secretly training Chechen rebels in sophisticated terror techniques to enable them to carry out more effective attacks against Russian forces."[42]

Yet Iran's ability to influence its neighbors to the north does not depend exclusively on its ability or willingness to threaten their vital interests. While its conventional weapons and deployable terrorist and insurgent groups are always on the table; they rarely are brandished publicly, at least among Iran's neighbors. In its day-to-day relations with its neighbors, Iran's regional belligerence has given way to a charm offensive designed to create allies through the institution of high-level contacts with its Transcaucasian and Central Asian neighbors, including Afghanistan, and the invocation of major trade, transportation, and energy deals.[43] These ties include joint cooperation against terrorism with Turkey, the provision of energy (including electricity) to Armenia, Georgia, Tajikistan, and Afghanistan, and the importation of energy from Kazakhstan and Turkmenistan.[44] The point of this strategy is to create enduring political and economic ties so that its northern neighbors, including Turkey, will think twice before allowing America to deploy any form of military power to the Caspian region, lest those states lose valuable political and economic ties with Iran as a result.

Hard choices

The foregoing assessment underscores just how difficult it would be for the United States to build, sustain and justify an allied military coalition against Iran, either from NATO or from the former Soviet states. It also highlights just how constrained the options of the U.S. are, in no small measure thanks to its own policies in Iraq and their consequences. But against any effort to rule out a forceful effort to stop Iranian nuclearization, it is necessary to weigh the consequences of allowing Iran to succeed in developing a usable nuclear weapon capability.

Accordingly, the U.S. should work to improve military-technical cooperation with regional friends and allies, by deepening existing bilateral military relationships where feasible (with Turkey, the Gulf Cooperation Council (GCC) states, and the Central Asian Republics), forging new bilateral security relationships where possible (with Iraq and Afghanistan), and pursuing regional cooperative ventures where desirable (such as augmenting efforts already underway to create shared air- and missile defense, early warning and C4I arrangements). Such an approach, though certainly less appealing than creating new regional political and security structures, would allow the U.S. to build on existing bilateral and multilateral efforts and, through incremental steps, lay the foundation for future regional collective security arrangements.[45]

Today Iran, with some merit, believes that it can defy the will of the United Nations and count on Moscow and Beijing to prevent forceful international action against it.[46] It has every reason to think that it can violate the NPT with impunity, and challenge the UN and the strongest alliance in the world without consequence. Such a violation would represent a threat not only to vital American and allied interests in the Middle East, but to the entire principle of international order as well.[47] Successful Iranian defiance would torpedo the NPT and its associated legal regime. It would also deal a body blow to arms control writ large, demonstrating that existing nonproliferation efforts are unable and unwilling to impose penalties upon violators, no matter how public and egregious the violation.

Unfortunately, history suggests that such threats to international security can only be successfully dealt with forcefully, as in the cases of Nazi Germany and Imperial Japan. The same holds true with regard to Iran; if the international community cannot stop this threat through political means, it will need to act militarily, and to do so before Iran can harness its newfound capabilities. While a large percentage of politics consists of trying to playing a bad hand well, no one will forgive the governments of our time for failing to play this hand, much less playing it well and in time.

ENDNOTES

1. Bill Samii, "New Formula, Same Result," *Asia Times*, August 24, 2006, http://www.atimes.com/atimes/Middle_East/HH24Ak02.html; Gareth Porter, "US Made an Offer Iran Can Only Refuse," *Asia Times*, August 24, 2006, http://www.atimes.com/atimes/Middle_East/HH24Ak01.html.

2. Kamal Nazer Yasin, "The Results of the Lebanese War Embolden Iran on Nuclear Issue," *Eurasia Insight*, August 24, 2006, http://www.eurasianet.org/departments/insight/articles/eav082406.shtml; George Perkovich, "Iran's Lebanon Card," Yale-Global.com, August 25, 2006, www.yaleglobal.yale.edu/display.article?id=8052; Michael Slackman, "Saying it Is Not a Threat, Iran Opens a Heavy-Water Reactor,' *New York Times*, August 27, 2006, 10.

3. Steven Lee Myers, "Russia Says It Opposes U.N. Sanctions on Iran," *New York Times*, August 26, 2006, A6.

4. "Major Powers Warn Iran on Nuclear Programme," *Times of London*, March 30, 2006, http://www.timesonline.co.uk/article/0,,3-2111093,00.html.

5. Roland Dannreuther, "The Middle East: Toward a Substantive European Role in the Peace Process." in Roland Dannreuther, ed., *European Union Foreign and Security policy: Towards a Neighborhood Strategy* (London: Routledge, 2004), 152.

6. Wolfgang Wagner, "The Democratic Legitimacy of European Security and Defence Policy," European Union Institute for Security Studies *Occasional Paper* no. 57 (2005), 26.

7. Seymour Hersch, "The Last Stand," New Yorker, July 10-17, 2006, 42-49; Sarah Baxter and Uzi Mahnaimi, "NATO May Help US Airstrikes on Iran," *Sunday Times* (London), March 5, 2006; *Tagespiegel* (Berlin), December 28, 2005; William M. Arkin, "The Pentagon Preps for Iran, " *Washington Post*, April 16, 2006, B16.

8. Douglas T. Stuart and William Tow, *The Limits of Alliance: NATO Out-of-Area Problems Since 1949* (Baltimore: Johns Hopkins University Press, 1990).

9. Philip Gordon, "NATO's Growing Role in the Greater Middle East," Emirates Center for Strategic Studies and Research *Emirates Lecture Series* no. 63, 2006.

10. "NATO Seeking New Partners to Broaden Area of Operations," Agence France Presse, July 6, 2006; Riad Kahwaji, "NATO Seeks Larger Role in Volatile Middle East,' *Defense News*, December 6, 2004, 18.

11. Michael Cox, "Beyond the West: Terrors in Transatlantia," *European Journal of International Relations* XI, no. 2 (2005), 203-233; Daniel N. Nelson, "Three Fictions of Transatlantic Relations," in Heinz Gaertner and Ian M. Cuthbertson, eds., *European Security and Transatlantic Relations After 9/11 and the Iraq War* (New York; Palgrave Macmillan, 2006), 119-125.

^{12.} "Iran; A Test for the Great Powers," *Russia in Global Affairs* 2, no. 1 (2004); Kimberley L. Thachuk, "Countering Terrorism Across the Atlantic?" National Defense University Center for Technology and National Security Policy *Defense Horizons* no. 53, July 2006, http://www.ndu.edu/ctnsp/defense_horizons/FINAL_DH_53.pdf; Adam Ward, "Shaping the Choices of Countries at Strategic Crossroads," presentation at the National Defense University Symposium on "Implementing the 2006 Quadrennial Defense Review (QDR)," Washington, DC, March 16, 2005.

^{13.} Michael Eisenstadt, "The Challenges of U.S. Preventive Action," in Henry Sokolski and Patrick Clawson, eds., *Checking Iran's Nuclear Ambitions* (Carlisle Barracks, PA: Strategic Studies institute, US Army War College, 2004), 121.

^{14.} Walter Posch, "Conclusion: A Triple Track Policy for the EU?" in Walter Posch, ed., "Iranian Challenges," Institute for Security Studies of the European Union *Chaillot Paper* no. 89 (2006), 128. While this may seem an amazing statement when fully understood, it certainly reflects a well-established point of view in Europe.

^{15.} Nicole Gnesotto, "La PESC, Entre Iran et la Constitution," Institute for Security Studies of the European Union *Bulletin IESUE* no. 19, 2006; See also Walter Posch, "Dialogue With Iran: The EU Way out of the Impasse."

^{16.} Ibid., 21; Ivo Daalder, Nicole Gnesotto, and Philip Gordon, eds., *Crescent of Crisis; U.S.-European Strategy for the Greater Middle East* (Washington and Paris: Brookings Institution Press and the European Union institute for Security Studies, 2006).

^{17.} "A Secure Europe in a Better World," European Security Strategy, Brussels, Belgium, December 12, 2003, http://www.consilium.europa.eu/uedocs/cms Upload/78367.pdf.

^{18.} Wagner, 17-19, 26-28; Lindstrom, 22.

^{19.} "A Secure Europe in a Better World," European Security Strategy.

^{20.} James Sperling, "Capabilities Traps and Gaps: Symptom or Cause of a Troubled Transatlantic Relationship?" *Contemporary Security Policy*, XXV, no. 3 (2004), 465-466.

^{21.} Ibid.

^{22.} Ibidem, 466.

^{23.} Lindstrom, 51-57; Peter Van Ham and Richard L. Kugler, "Western Unity and the Transatlantic Security Challenge," George C. Marshall European Center for Security Studies *Marshall Center Papers* no. 4 (2004), 23.

^{24.} Rob de Wijk, "The Implications for Force Transformation: The Small Country Perspective," in Daniel S. Hamilton, ed., *Transatlantic Transformations: Equipping NATO for the 21st Century* (Washington: Center for Transatlantic Relations, Johns Hopkins University, 2004), 117.

25. Michael E. O'Hanlon, *Defense Strategy for the Post-Saddam Era* (Washington: Brookings Institution Press, 2005), 64-69.

26. "Putin Will Try to Keep U.S. Military Out of Tajikistan: Report," Agence France Presse, October 5, 2005; "'No' to US Base in Tajikistan," Center for Eastern Studies *Eastweek* no. 11, September 20, 2005; Luigi Ippolito, "Rice's Great 'Central Asian Game,'" *Corriere Della Sera* (Milan), October 13, 2005.

27. "Tajik-US Relations must not Be 'Overvalued,'" *Asia-Plus* (Dushanbe), July 17, 2006.

28. *Radio Free Europe/Radio Liberty Newsline* 9, no. 191 (2005), http://www.rferl.org/newsline/2005/10/111005.asp.

29. "Russia to Pressure Disloyal CIS Countries," *Nezavisimaya Gazeta* (Moscow), October 13, 2005.

30. "Jiang Deplores Expansion of Anti-Terror War," *The News International* (Pakistan), April 22, 2002; Itar-TASS (Moscow), February 12, 2002; Igor Ivanov, "Guiding Principles of Russia's Foreign Policy," *Kommersant-Vlast* (Moscow), June 11, 2002.

31. Fariz Ismailzade, "Azerbaijan Under Iranian and Russian Pressure on Relations to U.S.," Johns Hopkins University Central Asia-Caucasus Institute *Central Asia-Caucasus Analyst*, November 3, 2004, http://www.cacianalyst.org/view_article.php?articleid=2797; Oleg Komotsky, "Ilham Aliyev Supports Iran," *Novye Izvestiya* (Moscow), August 25, 2005.

32. IRNA (Tehran), May 16, 2005.

33. *Ayna* (Baku), December 6, 2005; Interfax-Kazakhstan (Almaty), October 1, 2005; *Radio Free Europe/Radio Liberty Newsline* 10, no. 111 (2006), *http://www.rferl.org/newsline/2006/06/190606.asp.*

34. Marat Yermukanov, "Kazakhstan Seeks Iran's Reconciliation With the West," Jamestown Foundation *Eurasia Daily Monitor* iss. 116, June 19, 2006, http://www.jamestown.org/edm/article.php?article_id=2371193.

35. "Iran Says US Should Recognize it as a "Big, Regional Power,'" Associated Press, April 7, 2006.

36. Ariel Cohen, "Iran's Claim Over Caspian Sea Resources Threaten Energy Security," Heritage Foundation *Backgrounder* no. 1582, September 4, 2002, http://www.heritage.org/Research/MiddleEast/upload/20785_1.pdf.

37. Michael Lelyveld, "Caspian: Conflicts Likely at President's Summit," *Eurasia Insight*, April 20, 2002, http://www.eurasianet.org/departments/insight/articles/pp042002.shtml.

38. Anthony H. Cordesman, *Iran's Developing Military Capabilities* (Washington: Center for Strategic & International Studies, 2006), 43-48, 64-65.

39. Ibid., 83, 94-96.

40. Ariel Cohen, "Yankees in the Heartland: US policy in Central Asia After 9/11," in Ariel Cohen, ed., *Eurasia in Balance: the US and the Regional Power Shift* (Aldershot: Ashgate Publishers, 2005), 89-90.

41. Ilan Berman, "Tackling the Moscow-Tehran Connection," *The Journal of International Security Affairs* no. 10, Spring 2006, 76-77.

42. Ibid.; Ilan Berman, *Tehran Rising: Iran's Challenge to the United States* (Lanham: Rowman & Littlefield, 2005), 95.

43. Itar-TASS (Moscow), June 11, 2004; Dmitry Vekhoturov, "Iran Recognizes Tajikistan As Equal Partner," *Avesta* (Dushanbe), October 31, 2005; *Uzbek Television Second Channel* (Tashkent), May 18, 2004.

44. "Petropars Eyeing Joint Turkmenistan Projects With Petronas NOC," International Institute for Caspian Studies *Newsletter*, January 15, 2006 ; "Iran Planning to Raise Import of Kazakh Oil," *Alexander's Gas & Oil Connections* XI, no. 12 (2006); "Iran and Tajikistan Increase Political and Economic Cooperation," *Jane's intelligence Review*, March 2006.

45. Michael Eisenstadt, "Deter and Contain: Dealing with a Nuclear Iran," Testimony before the House Armed Services Committee, February 1, 2006, http://www.house. gov/hasc/2-1-06Eisenstadt.pdf.

46. Perkovich; Myers; Yasin, "The Results of the Lebanese War Embolden Iran on Nuclear Issue."

47. Mark Fitzpatrick, "Assessing Iran's Nuclear Programme," *Survival* XLVIII, no. 3 (2006), 25-26.

COUNTERPROLIFERATION CHALLENGES

Robert L. Pfaltzgraff, Jr.

Even though it has been unable to do so thus far, the United States remains committed to preventing Iran from becoming a nuclear weapons state. Back in 2003, President Bush declared publicly that the United States "would not tolerate" the emergence of a nuclear armed Iran.[1] Since then, he and other Administration officials have reiterated this conviction.[2] In its March 2006 National Security Strategy, the White House officially identified why, citing the proliferation of nuclear weapons as the most important national security threat confronting the United States, and Iran as the greatest state-based challenge to American interests.[3]

To be sure, America's political differences with Iran extend well beyond the nuclear issue. Today, the United States is deeply concerned by Iran's extensive support for terrorist organizations worldwide, including Hezbollah in Lebanon, Hamas and Islamic Jihad in Gaza and the West Bank, and even al-Qaeda. Tehran is also playing a destabilizing role in Iraq, providing military assistance to Shi'ite militias in the South and in the process contributing significantly to the ongoing violence there. An additional source of tension is Iran's dismal human rights record, punctuated by summary executions, torture, arbitrary arrests and detention, discrimination against women, intimidation of the media, and efforts to eliminate regime opponents.

But the problem of Iran's nuclear program is particularly grave because it exists within a broader context. The inability to stop Iran from acquiring a nuclear capability has provoked anxiety among Tehran's neighbors and triggered an acceleration in the nuclear programs of its

Sunni-dominated regional competitors.[4] This sort of expanded proliferation, in turn, will increase the likelihood that such weapons could fall into terrorist hands. Of added concern is the international precedent being set by Iran's nuclear advances. Simply put, Iran's progress is proof positive that the peaceful nuclear energy opportunities provided to signatories of the 1968 Nuclear Nonproliferation Treaty (NPT) can lay the groundwork for the rapid acquisition of a nuclear weapons capability. With additional states likely to follow suit, traditional constraints on proliferation are likely to come under heavy strain in the near future.

Washington is certainly not alone in these concerns. A broad international consensus has begun to emerge about the threat posed by Iran's activities. As German Foreign Minister Joschka Fischer put it in May 2006: "There can no longer be any reasonable doubt that Iran's ambition is to obtain a nuclear weapons capability."[5] Even critics of the Iraq war, openly skeptical of American intentions in the region, have rallied behind international efforts to confront Tehran over its clandestine nuclear activities.[6] Yet on a practical level, there as yet exists no comprehensive counterproliferation strategy capable of keeping the world's most dangerous weapons out of the hands of the world's most dangerous regime.

The state of American strategy

Over the past several decades, American policymakers have focused their efforts to prevent nuclear proliferation on cutting off access to fissile material, the essential ingredient for a nuclear weapon.[7] This has led to what are essentially two parallel efforts: (1) to keep states from obtaining the means to produce fissile materials for nuclear weapons; and (2) to make it difficult or impossible to transfer these materials to rogue states or non-state actors. Today, both initiatives warrant a serious rethink.

On the first front, that of limiting fissile material production, Iran stands as a test case for the deficiencies inherent in the contemporary nuclear nonproliferation regime. Upon their accession to the NPT, non-nuclear countries are granted the right to pursue nuclear energy for peaceful purposes, such as electricity generation. In effect, this has meant that signatories—Iran among them—are unrestrained in testing the nuclear weapons threshold with the "legal" development of the necessary fuel-cycle capacity. As a result, the Iranian regime has been able, as part of its ostensibly peaceful nuclear program, to enrich and reprocess uranium on its own initiative—all while denying the International Atomic

Energy Agency the necessary access to verify compliance with its NPT commitments.[8]

With regard to the second problem, it has become apparent that efforts aimed at keeping fissile material out of the hands of rogue states and terrorists have been equally undermined by the Iranian regime. For more than two decades, the Islamic Republic has been the beneficiary of extensive nuclear and ballistic missile assistance from a variety of nuclear suppliers, chief among them Russia, China, and North Korea. (Until it was uncovered and dismantled in late 2003, the clandestine nuclear network of Pakistani scientist Abdul Qadeer Khan also served as a major source of nuclear hardware and know-how to Iran, as well as other countries.)

Russia's contribution centers on the 1000 megawatt light-water reactor now nearing completion at the southern Iranian city of Bushehr. Moscow has also provided the Iranian regime with training in reactor operations, laser equipment for uranium enrichment, and help for heavy water and nuclear-grade graphite production.[9] China, for its part, has supplied Iran with critical nuclear and ballistic missile technology, as well as missiles themselves.[10] As for North Korea, it has played a key role in the development of Iran's advanced "Shahab-3" medium-range missile,[11] and is currently believed to be engaged in cooperative nuclear development with the Islamic Republic.[12] Iran has also been a beneficiary of the infamous AQ Khan nuclear network, obtaining blueprints—as well as possibly hardware, manufacturing, and nuclear procurement capabilities—from the illicit cartel over the span of a decade and a half.[13]

To its credit, the Bush administration has become acutely aware of these failings. Since taking office in 2001, it has embarked upon an ambitious effort to reconfigure American nonproliferation policy to better respond to emerging threats and "bad faith" actors such as Iran.

This effort includes the Global Threat Reduction Initiative (GTRI), launched in mid-2004 and designed to locate, track, secure, reduce, remove, and dispose of existing stockpiles of nuclear material through a variety of methods.[14] So far, the GTRI has succeeded in converting 39 nuclear reactors located in dozens of countries, including the United States, from using weapons-grade highly enriched uranium (HEU) to low enriched uranium (LEU) useful only in peaceful nuclear generation. Similarly, this program has resulted in the return to Russia of roughly 148 kilograms of HEU from former Soviet client states and satellites (including Libya and Romania), as well as the repatriation of U.S.-supplied nuclear materials from Germany.[15]

President Bush's agenda also includes the Proliferation Security Initiative (PSI), a watershed nonproliferation effort designed to enhance international cooperation in the interdiction of WMD shipments by sea, land and air. Its most notable success was the 2003 interception of the BBC China, a German-owned vessel bound for Libya carrying a cargo of nuclear centrifuges. That discovery—coupled with the credible threat of force from Washington—led directly to Libyan strongman Muammar Qaddafi's renunciation of his nuclear program, and set in motion the chain of events that dismembered the AQ Khan network. In addition to its role in Libya's nuclear reversal, the PSI, with strong support from Japan as a core member, has significantly impeded North Korea's illicit nuclear and ballistic missile trade.

A third such effort is Caspian Guard. Launched in 2003, Caspian Guard is a bilateral security assistance effort encompassing counter-proliferation, counterterrorism, anti-trafficking and resource protection between the United States and two former Soviet republics: Azerbaijan and Kazakhstan. Over the past three-and-a-half years, the U.S. European Command (EUCOM), working together with civilian and private-sector entities, has bolstered its security relationship with both states through stepped-up counterproliferation capabilities and joint exercises. By 2011, the United States will have spent some $135 million on "Caspian Guard"-related projects designed to enhance the effectiveness of crisis response in the region.[16]

Doing better

These initiatives unquestionably represent the first steps toward a more aggressive, more robust counterproliferation policy. Yet, when it comes to confronting the complex proliferation challenge posed by Iran, much more work still needs to be done.

As noted above, Iran's WMD effort has received from a number of foreign countries, which have invested a great deal of resources, financial aid, and even manpower in assisting Tehran's nuclear program and boosting its ballistic missile capabilities. This is in and of itself a cause for concern. Of perhaps even greater significance, however, is the likelihood of onward proliferation of these nuclear and weapons technologies to both state and non-state actors. Such worries are well-founded. Over the past several years, for example, Iran has emerged as a major source of ballistic missile assistance for the regime of Bashar al-Assad in Syria.[17] Likewise, the Iranian regime has passed on cutting edge technology to

Lebanon's Hezbollah terrorist organization for use against Israel; during the July-August 2006 Israel-Hezbollah war, for example, the Shi'ite militia disabled an Israeli warship using an Iranian variant of the Chinese C-802 "Silkworm"—a missile that Israeli officials previously did not know Hezbollah possessed.[18] Iran's leaders, moreover, have made clear that they view weapons of mass destruction as an export commodity. Iran's Supreme Leader, the Ayatollah Ali Khamenei, stated publicly that the Islamic Republic is prepared to transfer the [nuclear] experience, knowledge and technology of its scientists" to its friends and allies.[19]

In response, the United States needs a truly multidimensional American counterproliferation strategy—one that involves components of defense, denial, and dismantlement.

Defense

Today, as a result of Iran's efforts to acquire nuclear weapons, the United States and its allies face a growing threat of nuclear attack, either by missile or as a result of terrorist use. Concerted efforts are needed to provide defenses against both types of threat.

In the case of missiles, this necessitates the deployment of an operational missile defense system with a truly global capability. The goal of the United States should be to make the development and use of missiles by the Iranian regime more costly and potentially prohibitive, and to do so through the demonstrated ability to counter such deployments. In practice, this means assuring that we can augment a robust missile defense more easily than the Iranian regime can build new missile systems capable of penetrating such defenses. This type of system should be geared toward dissuading Iran from deploying missiles with WMD-capable warheads and deterring Tehran from launching missiles against Israel and other U.S allies in the region or, more directly, at the continental United States. Such a global missile defense "shield" would be best served by a space-based interceptor capability that provides for multiple interception opportunities during a missile's flight.[20]

Equally important, however, is the ability of the U.S. to develop technologies capable of detecting and thwarting the shipment of nuclear systems or their components to terrorist with cells operating either within the United States or within striking distance of U.S. assets abroad. Port security therefore is a major priority; without an adequate base of resources and up-to-date technologies, America's ports will remain the Achilles heel through which Hezbollah and like-minded groups can potentially mount a devastating terrorist attack.

Denial

Simultaneously, the United States must work more effectively to deny Iran the offensive technology it seeks. However progressive they might be, the Bush administration's counterproliferation initiatives currently fall short in this regard on a number of fronts. The PSI, for example, currently does not encompass at least two of Iran's neighbors, Qatar and Saudi Arabia, severely limiting its effectiveness in and around the Persian Gulf. Likewise, the PSI and Caspian Guard operate largely independent of one another, failing to coordinate policy on what in many cases are common proliferation patterns. Greater international collaboration, therefore, is essential; initiatives such as PSI and Caspian Guard should be strengthened and their membership expanded. They should also coordinate their efforts to the fullest extent possible, providing an integrated response to both north-south (from the former Soviet Union to Iran) and south-north (via the Gulf) proliferation.

Another area of critical focus is diversification. Today, much of America's counterproliferation strategy centers on successful maritime interdictions. Such a focus is logical, given that the principal target of the PSI thus far has been North Korea. Iran, on the other hand, receives inputs by land and air, in addition to by sea. As a result, it is essential to expand existing counterproliferation and interdiction mechanisms to address more fully technology transfers via land and air routes from North and Northeast Asia. In this regard the countries of Central Asia have a crucial role to play; because of their strategic location between Iran and its principal ballistic missile supplier, these nations have the ability to choke off potential smuggling routes between the DPRK and the Islamic Republic, or between Iran and entities in the Russian Federation.

Dismantlement

The United States must also consider the possibility that, should the previous two options fail, it could be necessary to dismantle Iran's nuclear capabilities by force. Because such an option carries serious risks,[21] military force must remain a policy of last resort. However, if and when it is attempted, the options for such action will fall into three general categories.

The first is the use of force aimed primarily at isolating the Islamic Republic from its external sources of support. The principal goal of such an effort—manifested in the form of a blockade or quarantine—would be to prevent Iran from gaining access to nuclear-related technologies from proliferators such as North Korea or Russia. Moreover, the effort could be expanded to limit Iran's ability to export oil or to import refined petroleum products for its own energy needs. Either exercise is likely to have a profound effect on the dysfunctional Iranian economy. An important secondary objective of such an effort would be to prevent onward proliferation from Iran, prohibiting the regime from exporting nuclear technology to third countries or non-state terrorist proxies. Whether such an effort, enforced by the United States Navy and our allies, would have its intended effect could not, however, be easily foreseen. Success would depend largely upon unknown variables, such as the extent to which Tehran remains dependent on external inputs for progress on its nuclear weapons program.

The second set of options available to the United States is military strikes designed to complement parallel, non-military measures, chief among them economic sanctions. The former would be directed against Iran's energy infrastructure, and encompass not only strikes against Iranian maritime forces (to prevent them from interrupting tanker traffic), but also the targeting of refineries, oil and gas pipelines, and tanker terminals. Iran's energy infrastructure is located almost exclusively in its west, with facilities at Abadan, Kangan, Shiraz, and Bandar Abbas.[22] Together with Iran's oil and gas pipelines and its extensive network of offshore facilities, these targets remain relatively "soft" and vulnerable to attack or sabotage. The goal of such efforts would be to enhance the effectiveness of international pressure on the Iranian economy, thereby making the regime incapable of sustaining its drive for nuclear weapons.

The third and most severe scenario involves direct military strikes against Iranian nuclear facilities. Operations against nuclear targets could be mounted with air power as well as special operations forces deployed clandestinely in Iran. But because much of Iran's nuclear infrastructure is scattered, fortified and hidden from view, the full success of this type of military action could not be assured in advance. It is widely assumed that an option similar to that launched in 1981 by Israel against the Iraqi nuclear facility at Osirak could not be undertaken today with an equal measure of success.[23] Although we know the location of many of Iran's nuclear sites—among them Bushehr, Natanz, Arak, and Isfahan—significant aspects of the Iranian nuclear complex remain unknown. And in the absence of key information, it is impossible to ascertain how greatly the Iranian program could be set back by military action. Furthermore, whether the United States would be prepared, both politically and psychologically, to attack Iranian nuclear sites remains an open question.

The key variable influencing all of these options is time. The longer the world has until Iran "goes nuclear," the greater the opportunity to dissuade Iran from its present course—or at least to prepare a strategy to counter a nuclear-armed Iran.

Complicating this equation is the issue of how Tehran acquires these capabilities. Most intelligence estimates are based on the assumption that Iran will import the technologies, including hardware and know-how that will eventually lead to more advanced regime capabilities. Generally, these estimates have put the nuclear weapons "threshold" at between 5 to 10 years. But these assessments usually ignore the possibility that Iran could obtain a complete warhead or substantial components for a completed nuclear weapon from an outside source—a development that would dramatically shorten the time the Iranian regime would need to field a usable nuclear weapon. After all, Iran is doing more than simply working on indigenous uranium enrichment and reprocessing. It is also engaged in a serious effort to acquire fissile material and nuclear components from abroad. The result could be an Iranian nuclear weapon far sooner than the intelligence community has predicted.

A related question is exactly how quickly Tehran's latent weapons capability could be activated to produce an actual nuclear weapon. Iran's mastery of the nuclear fuel cycle would make it a virtual nuclear-weapons-capable state, requiring only the means to manufacture warheads and delivery systems.

Thinking beyond Tehran

It is not at all clear that American counterproliferation efforts, however robust, can provide the necessary solution to Iran's nuclear ambitions. Indeed, there is ample reason to believe that the Iranian regime is so determined to acquire nuclear weapons that no amount of U.S. and international pressure will be sufficient to prompt its leaders to reverse course. As a result, American policymakers must simultaneously consider methods to prevent Iran from acquiring such technology, and ways to prevent Iran's leaders from using the technology they have already acquired, either directly or via proliferation to other countries or terrorist groups.

The mere possession of nuclear weapons undoubtedly will make the Iranian regime a more formidable adversary for the United States and its allies. But Iran's nuclearization will also reverberate throughout the greater Middle East, setting off a dangerous chain reaction that will severely strain existing alliances and, ultimately, the contemporary non-proliferation regime itself. At issue, therefore, is not whether Washington can countenance the emergence of one atomic Middle Eastern power, but of many. Sadly, unless serious efforts are made to strengthen and expand current counterproliferation initiatives, such a state of affairs seems all but inevitable in the years ahead.

ENDNOTES

1. David E. Sanger, "Bush Says U.S. Will Not Tolerate Building of Nuclear Arms by Iran," *New York Times*, June 19, 2003, 1.

2. Barry Schweid, "Bush Won't Allow a Nuclear-Armed Iran," Associated Press, September 5, 2006.

3. White House, Office of the Press Secretary, *The National Security Strategy of the United States of America*, March 2006, 20. The document declares: "Any government that chooses to be an ally of terror, such as Syria or Iran, has chosen to be an enemy of freedom, justice, and peace. The world must hold those regimes to account."

3. Indeed, there already are signs that Iran's neighbors, fearful of a shift in the regional balance of power, are contemplating strategic counterweights to an Iranian "bomb." Richard Beeston, "Six Arab States Join Rush to go Nuclear," *Times of London*, November 4, 2006.

4. Joschka Fischer, "The Case for Bargaining with Iran," *Washington Post*, May 29, 2006.

5. See, for example, Richard Beeston, "Saudis Warn Iran That its Nuclear Plan Risks Disaster," *Times of London*, January 16, 2006.

6. See, for example, Graham Allison, *Nuclear Terrorism: the Ultimate Preventable Catastrophe* (New York: Henry Holt and Company, 2004), esp. 143-175.

7. According to the September 13, 2006 report of the IAEA Director General, Iran has taken none of the steps that the Board deemed necessary a year earlier, and again in February 2006. The quality of Iran's cooperation with the Agency has seriously declined. Iran has failed to comply with UN Security Council Resolution 1696… Iran refused the Agency's access to operating records at the Pilot Fuel Enrichment Plant at Natanz. Iran also continues to decline remote monitoring and initially declined the Agency's request to carry out a Design Information Verification visit.

8. Valerie Lincy, "Iran Defies the Security Council, Again," Wisconsin Project on Nuclear Arms Control *Iran Watch*, September 1, 2006, 7-8.

9. Ibid., 9.

10. Joseph Bermudez, "A History of Ballistic Missile Development in the DPRK," Monterrey Institute for International Studies Center for Nonproliferation Studies *Occasional Paper* no. 2 (1999), http://cns.miis.edu/pubs/opapers/op2/op2.pdf.

11. See, for example, "Iran Expands Nuke Cooperation with N. Korea," Middle East Newsline, June 13, 2003, http://www.menewsline.com/stories/2003/june/06_13_1.html.

[11.] John Wilson, "Iran, Pakistan, and Nukes," *Washington Times*, October 4, 2005, http://www.washtimes.com/op-ed/20041004-015707-2087rhtm.

[12.] "Department of Energy Launches New Global Threat Reduction Initiative," U.S. Department of Energy Press Release, May 26, 2004, http://www.energy.gov/news/1359.htm.

[13.] "Global Threat Reduction Initiative: Fact Sheet," IAEA, http://www-pub.iaea.org/MTCD/Meetings/PDFplus/2004/cn139fact.pdf.

[14.] "Pentagon Plans to Extend Caspian Guard Program," *Baku Today*, December 18, 2005, http://www.bakutoday.net/view.php?d=14417.

[15.] Ilan Berman, *Tehran Rising: Iran's Challenge to the United States* (Lanham: Rowman & Littlefield, 2005), 50.

[16.] Alon Ben-David, "Hizbullah Hits Israel's INS Hanit With Anti-Ship Missile," *Jane's Defence Weekly*, July 18, 2006, http://www.janes.com/defence/news/jdw/jdw060718_1_n.shtml.

[17.] Nazila Fathi, "Iran Says It Will Share Nuclear Skills," *New York Times*, April 25, 2006, http://www.nytimes.com/2006/04/25/world/middleeast/25cnd-iran.html?ex=1303617600&en=78525f46bcf67177&ei=5088&partner=rssnyt&emc=rss.

[18.] For an extensive discussion of space-based missile defense, see *Final Report of the Independent Working Group on Missile Defense, the Space Relationship, and the Twenty-First Century* (Cambridge, MA: Institute for Foreign Policy Analysis, 2006).

[19.] A military attack on Iran could be met with several debilitating responses. While Iran's conventional military is no match for that of the U.S., it does possess significant asymmetric capabilities, including, but is not limited to, a closure of the Strait of Hormuz, activation of terrorist assets against the U.S. homeland and American interests abroad, as well as ballistic missile attacks against U.S. forces stationed in the Middle East. A military attack could also result in a "rally around the flag" effect, galvanizing public support behind the Iranian regime. Such a military operation would also likely further strain America's already overstretched military resources, leaving the United States vulnerable in other theaters.

[20.] Department of Energy, Energy Information Administration, "Country Analysis Brief: Iran," August 2006, http://www.eia.doe.gov/emeu/cabs/Iran/pdf.pdf.

[21.] Richard K. Betts, "The Osirak Fallacy," *The National Interest* no. 83, Spring 2006, http://www.ciaonet.org/olj/ni/ni_sp06/ni_sp06c.html.

[22.] "Analysts Say a Nuclear Iran Is Years Away," *New York Times*, April 13, 2006, http://www.nytimes.com/2006/04/13/world/middleeast/13iran.html?ex=1302580800&en=20def7e680059030&ei=5090&partner=rssuscrland&emc=rss.

23. For more on Iranian acquisition activities and U.S. intelligence shortfalls, see Ilan Berman, "Iran's Atomic Effort," *Washington Times*, June 9, 2006.

Planning for Conflict

John F. Sigler

"Never get involved in a land war in Asia," the old adage goes. Yet, if one considers the Global War on Terrorism, or GWOT as it is commonly termed, the United States is currently involved in three such wars: Iraq, Afghanistan and other counterterrorism operations in the theater. Ground action against Iran represents a potential fourth front. Although Iran's nuclear efforts have been on the national security agenda for over a decade, now they are receiving broad public attention because, by all indications, the Iranian regime is fast closing in on a key strategic prize: a nuclear weapons capability coupled with accurate, long-range delivery systems.

When considering options *vis-à-vis* Iran, American military planners generally have focused on two major variables. The first is the "lessons learned" by the Iranian regime concerning nuclear weapons over the past two decades. These include: the powerful deterrent and bargaining positions afforded even to otherwise insignificant nations (and Iran is not insignificant); that international penalties can be overcome, particularly by an oil-rich nation during a time of high prices; and that the best way to safeguard its program is to make it hidden, inaccessible and redundant. As a result, Iran's nuclear effort today is geographically and functionally diversified. Key elements are deeply buried in hardened underground facilities, and not all facility locations are known.

The second major variable is the Persian psyche itself. A country tremendously proud of its heritage, intensely nationalistic, and which sees itself as the center, protector and exporter of the Shi'a form of Islam, Iran has hegemonic designs over the Persian Gulf. Therefore, it perceives tremendous value in the prestige and diplomatic leverage that accrue from possessing a nuclear weapons capability. Perhaps even more compelling is the threat the Iranian leadership perceives from the United States—as well as the emotional scars caused by the grinding eight-year war fought with Iraq during the 1980s. That Saddam Hussein's Ba'athist regime, an adversary which had fought Iranian forces to a standstill, was twice decisively vanquished by the United States now is seared into the Iranian national consciousness. As a result, many segments of the Iranian body politic, from hard-liners to moderates, now embrace their government's efforts to acquire a nuclear capability.

A decade ago, U.S. policy and military planners concluded that effective counterproliferation strikes against the Iranian nuclear program would be both extraordinarily challenging and costly on a number of levels. The challenges included incomplete intelligence, hardened and deeply buried targets, and the need to cause enough damage to prevent rapid reconstitution of the program. The likely costs included international condemnation, a reversal of internal Iranian movement—however glacial—toward reform, and a probable asymmetric response from Tehran, likely employing terrorist surrogates.

These conclusions certainly still apply today, but some things have changed. For one, the Iranian nuclear program is a decade closer to fruition. For another, the United States now is heavily engaged in other operations that are severely straining its armed forces. And, not insignificantly, a growing number of Muslims are concluding that Islam is the real American target. Military operations against Iran would certainly reinforce that perception, with potential second and third order effects elsewhere.

The current situation in Iraq in particular affects the strategic calculus of both countries. Iran is geographically larger, has a much larger population and arguably more capable armed forces than those possessed by the regime of Saddam Hussein prior to Operation Iraqi Freedom (especially in the areas of doctrine and command and control). The Iranians, who already knew the value of unconventional, asymmetric warfare—including the use of surrogates—against a large, first-rate army, have seen it amply and effectively demonstrated next door over the past three years. They are learning just what works and what does not—tactically, operationally and strategically—against the United States. Iran's leadership also is watching the changing state of the political debate in the United States, including the results of the 2006 mid-term elections, and is drawing its own conclusions.

The United States, meanwhile, is experiencing first-hand (and once again) one of the problems of a land war in Asia, bogging down into attrition warfare against a cunning and well-resourced asymmetric enemy. Perhaps the greatest asymmetry, however, is that while the U.S. is conducting operations at the tactical and operational level of warfare, the enemy is operating at the strategic level.

A number of writers today have consequently concluded that, while the use of force should be left on the table, it is not a good option and is best avoided in favor of any other approach.[1] Others have gone further, arguing that military options should be entirely discounted.[2] Still others have concluded that the first stages of operations against Iran are already in progress.[3]

To be sure, history is replete with examples of military victory followed by strategic defeat. But, setting aside whether action against the Iranian nuclear weapons program is a good idea, it is at least possible to identify the full range of military options open to the United States.

How America fights

In the U.S. armed forces, military planners follow a well-developed series of steps called the joint operational planning process. This is defined as "a coordinated joint staff procedure used by a commander to determine the best method of accomplishing assigned tasks and to direct the action necessary to accomplish the mission."[4] Within this process, if the planner has adequate time, a "deliberate plan" will be developed against the best estimate of what the future situation will look like.

This planning can take a year or more from start to finish. Major war plans and contingencies most often fall into this category. However, if the planner is faced with a more immediate threat, a "crisis action plan" can be developed over a period of weeks or days (sometimes even hours) to deal with a current or impending threat.

Iran, most likely, falls into the former camp. Presumably, the U.S. military has been directed to look in depth at Iran using the deliberate planning process. (Moreover, it does not appear, at least at this juncture, that a crisis action plan is immediately required—although that point certainly may be approaching.) The deliberate planning process includes:

- Receipt and analysis of the task(s) to be accomplished;

- Review of the enemy's situation and identification of additional essential information (intelligence) required;

- Development of alternative courses of action (COAs);

- Evaluation of the COAs and selection of the most optimal;

- Development of a detailed concept of operations for the desired COA and obtaining approval for it, and then;

- Preparation of a detailed plan, including necessary supporting plans.

The evaluation of the courses of action should have two major parts to it: first, an assessment of the military impact—the first order effects—and second, an evaluation of the geo-strategic impact—the second and third order effects—of each alternative. The first is performed by planners using a wide variety of techniques, including operations analysis and wargaming. The second can be performed by military commands utilizing officers with specialized regional training and experience, such as Army foreign area officers (FAOs) and, in the larger commands, political advisors (POLADS): senior diplomats seconded to the Department of Defense by the State Department. However, to understand and consider fully the strategic impact of each alternative, an interagency evaluation is by far the best approach. In reality, if one is actually conducted, such a survey is typically performed only on the selected option and is quite often accomplished by holding a major wargame with representatives of all agencies with a stake in the outcome (sometimes to include selected non-governmental organizations).

In any event, the first step of receiving and analyzing the mission is not trivial and is clearly the foundation upon which the plan must be based. On occasion, the National Command Authority may want to know what military options are available for differing missions. In that case, be multiple concept plans would need to be developed.

Planning options

What, then, are the potential missions for Iran? From "low end" to "high end," one possible set includes: show of force; coercive diplomacy; demonstration attacks; punitive strikes; counterproliferation operations; and, finally, regime replacement.

A *show of force* is an operation in response to an immediate threat or contingency, meant to deescalate the situation by showing both capability and resolve to respond. Should deescalation fail, the forces present then become the nucleus of the initial operational response. Sometimes the show of force can be accomplished by the mere presence of capable forces; often the available forces will conduct peacetime exercises that both showcase their capabilities and keep their readiness to respond at a high level. Stationing an air expeditionary wing into Qatar or the UAE for bilateral exercises, adding an additional carrier battle group to the Gulf, or ground force exercises in Kuwait are examples.

Coercive diplomacy is closely related to a show of force, but differentiated by the immediacy of the situation and the size of the response. When other forms of diplomacy are judged to be inadequate, or as not having had the desired effect, forces may be inserted into a region with the implication that they will be used should negotiations fail. There does not necessarily need to be an immediate crisis, as there is in a pure show of force, and the diplomatic goals are generally broader than simply deescalating a crisis. The United States has employed such "gunboat diplomacy" since its earliest days as a republic. In fairly recent times, the North Koreans have repeatedly rattled their sabers, often successfully, to achieve various bargaining positions.

A problem common to both a show of force and coercive diplomacy is the outcome when the adversary believes they are seeing a bluff and calls the hand. A tough decision—hopefully preplanned—is presented. Will the deployed forces actually be used? If so, how and what are the potential outcomes? The possibilities include escalation of a crisis in the case of a show of force, or perhaps creating a crisis in the case of coercive diplomacy. On the other hand, backing down once forces are deployed may significantly reduce both current bargaining positions and the leverage of such an option in the future. Another challenge is the "use it or lose it" problem; significant forces can only be forward-deployed in a ready but unengaged status for so long before they need to be returned to their home bases for crew rest and rotation, equipment maintenance and replacement and readiness training. During the coercive diplomacy phase prior to Operation Iraqi Freedom, U.S. force levels in the vicinity of Iraq rose to a level where they not only needed to be engaged or brought home within six to nine months of deployment, but the right mix of trained, ready forces to replace them at the same levels would not be available for some time.

Upping the ante from coercive diplomacy, *demonstration attacks* are actual or implied strike operations conducted to show the seriousness of the situation, imply additional commitment to use force and illustrate what more extensive, actual operations might look like. At the low end, they can be "mirror image" strikes against exercise targets on friendly territory near the potential scene of actual action. Terrain and targets are carefully chosen, and the strikes orchestrated and publicized in a manner that cannot be mistaken by the potential adversary. Mirror image attacks were used to great effect by both sides during the Cold War. At the high end of demonstrations, actual—albeit limited—strikes are conducted against selected enemy targets. The desired inference is that, absent acceptable resolution of the problem, major strikes will follow. Some political leaders may favor demonstrations as potentially limiting escalation; planners, however, usually do not recommend them because they have the potential to place friendly forces at risk without corresponding military impact.

The next step up the "escalation" ladder is *actual strikes* against various targets in response to unacceptable behavior, such as the violation of United Nations Security Council resolutions, an immediate and grave threat to vital interests, or the use of state-sponsored terrorism. The targets are often, but not necessarily, directly related to a particular behavior, and the usual norm is one of proportionality—in other words, let the punishment fit the crime. Quite often, therefore, these punitive strikes are limited in scope, and while locally or geographically effective, strategically they may have little value (the so-called "pin-prick" strikes against Iraq in the mid-1990s serve as a case in point). However, since the goal of punitive strikes may be not only retribution but dissuasion from further such behavior, the decision may be to respond with overwhelming force. The targets can be military, economic, infrastructure- or regime-related.

In this taxonomy of options the planner now arrives at the meat of options designed to slow down, stop or reverse a nation's nuclear weapons ambitions: *counterproliferation operations*. These are operations across the spectrum of warfare (from covert special operations through conventional air strikes and ground operations up to counter-nuclear strikes) that strike directly at an adversary's nuclear weapons and related programs. Ultimately there should be two goals: destroying (or at least significantly degrading) the program in question, and reversing the adversary's decision to pursue this program by raising his costs well above his perceived benefits. Two well-known examples of counterproliferation operations are the 1981 Israeli raid against the Osirak reactor and the four-day Operation Desert Fox carried out in 1999 by the U.S. Studying both can provide insights into what a counterproliferation operation against Iran, including attendant challenges and limitations, may look like.

One key limitation is that even fairly extensive operations, such as the 650 strike sorties over the four days of Operation Desert Fox, may only marginally delay a nation's weapons program. Desert Fox was estimated at the time to have slowed Saddam's program from less than a year to at most two years (although, to be fair, some writers now ascribe greater success to that operation).[5] Even Osirak, though commonly thought to be one of the most successful military operations of the modern era, did not completely destroy Saddam's programs or reverse his decision to possess nuclear weapons. Although the operation was, at the tactical and operational level, brilliantly conceived and executed, there is evidence that it, in fact, hardened Saddam's resolve and that the program actually accelerated as a result. Certainly, one result of that operation has been that Iranian leaders have designed their country's nuclear program to be "Osirak-proof."

This can lead to the highest level of violence on the planners' list of options: *regime replacement*. If the threat posed by a nation's nuclear weapons program is estimated to be potentially (or actually) devastating, then national command authorities are left with only four options: to find a diplomatic means to reverse the adversary's decision; to use military means to destroy or degrade the program to the point where time is gained and leverage increased to find an acceptable diplomatic solution; to replace a regime that will not forego its nuclear weapons program with a more compliant one, or; to learn to live with an adversary that poses a grave threat (as the United States and the Soviet Union did during the Cold War via an intricate deterrence regime that included the aptly-named concept of mutual assured destruction, MAD).

Regime replacement can occur in essentially two ways. It can be carried out by the nation's population, either through democratic processes or by force (coups, civil war or revolution). Alternatively, outside forces can effect such change by defeating with military force the existing regime and facilitating the installation of something else in its place. The latter option implies an invasion, the use of ground forces and some form of occupation until a new government is operational. A successful regime change might be defined as the establishment of a stable, reasonably compliant, successor government.

That definition, in turn, implies some period of stabilization until the new government is fully capable of governing, including the provision of a sufficient level of internal security. A key consideration here should be that the numbers required to topple the existing government may be significantly less that the numbers required to enforce order during the transition period. A 1999 analysis of stabilization requirements for Iraq, for example, was based roughly on the numbers of police required in both densely and lightly populated areas in other parts of the world. While combat objectives in Iraq could be achieved with reasonable risk with less than 150,000 Coalition ground forces, the foregoing analysis indicated that between 325,000 and 400,000 troops/police would be required to stabilize that nation of 27 million people.[6] By simple extrapolation, well over 800,000 might be required in Iran with its population of nearly 70 million. Not all of these forces need to be from the occupying coalition; in fact, it is preferable that they be, to the extent possible, competent police and armed forces from the nation itself. The imperative, of course, is that these forces are loyal to the nation, rather than to the former regime.

Envisioning military action

Given the scope and nature of what is known about the Iranian nuclear program, the following is representative of what a counterproliferation operation against Iran, short of regime replacement, might look like.[7]

Since most strategists believe that counterproliferation strikes will only be used should diplomacy fail, the initial deployment of forces would be a form of coercive diplomacy. Because U.S. forces are already heavily engaged in the region, the additional flow of personnel would have to be made evident to the Iranians. Alternatively, if strategists have concluded that coercive diplomacy will not work, the deployment phase could be accomplished under the cover of movements for the other operations currently underway in the theater, in order to maintain an element of surprise.

A potential combination of air forces could include 500 to 1,000 land and sea-based attack aircraft, supported by roughly 200 support aircraft of various types, including tanker, cargo, electronic, intelligence collection, command and control, search and rescue and special operations aircraft.[8] Naval forces also would contribute several thousand surface- and submarine-launched cruise missiles. Additional cruise missiles would be available on long-range Air Force bombers. Substantial numbers of unmanned drones, with a mix of real-time intelligence and electronic (as well as weapons delivery) capabilities, would also be employed. For counterproliferation operations, the primary combat-equipped ground forces would consist of joint special operations units; they might also include several special operations-capable Marine Corps units that could be deployed from amphibious ships to raid specific targets on Iranian-occupied islands and along to the Iranian coastline. Special operations missions can be generally classified as direct (offensive, usually covert missions against specific targets) or indirect (in support of other forces' missions—for example, target designation). Many of the Special Forces units with both direct and indirect missions would be covertly inserted into Iran prior to any opening attacks. A significant planning consideration here is the military and political cost associated with the compromise of any of the units operating within the adversary's borders.

If the operation is still about coercive diplomacy, planners might suggest weeks of intensive exercise sorties that would both demonstrate the seriousness of the situation and take the edge off the adversary's defensive readiness. On the night of the first attacks, Special Forces would move to their designated positions, while the initial long-range bombers sortie from bases as far away as Guam. Initial attacks by land- and sea-based aircraft, carried out against air defense targets, would be coordinated with cruise missile strikes against primary counterproliferation targets. Precision weapons would be employed to the maximum extent possible, both to maximize the probability of target neutralization per sortie and to minimize collateral damage. Follow-on attacks the first night and beyond would include sorties against known hardened and deeply-buried nuclear facilities using weapons as specified by the targeting experts. In some cases, target analysis may reveal mission-degrading weaknesses that can be attacked by more conventional precision weapons, while others would be judged vulnerable to the behemoth so-called "bunker busters." Still others—the most difficult to dismantle and destroy—may have to be attacked using highly-classified weapons and other technical means.[9] Another target set that would be discussed from the perspective of feasibility, effectiveness and legality would be key nuclear weapons program personnel, including directors, managers, scientists and engineers.

Counterproliferation targets would include nuclear laboratories, milling and mining facilities, processing and production plants, storage and transportation nodes as well as missile production and storage facilities. The first night's raid additionally would go after the highest value counter-force targets in order to blunt the potential Iranian response. Examples could include the Iranian regime's more capable aircraft, surface-to-surface missile installations, submarines and fast attack boats and associated support bases, as well as mine depots. Since the early 1990s, U.S. forces have worked hard to develop specialized weapons and tactics to target and destroy in near real-time enemy mobile surface-to-surface and ballistic missile launchers; some of the opening (and subsequent) sorties would, by necessity, be dedicated to that mission.[10]

The first twenty-four hours of attacks might be in the neighborhood of 200 to 300 sorties and Special Forces missions. Subsequent days might settle in at about 150 to 200 sorties per day. Battle damage assessment of the initial targets would be conducted, and repeat strikes assigned as necessary. Concurrently, the target set would be expanded to include political targets as directed by the National Command Authority. Such an operation, conducted over a six to twelve day period, should be successful in setting back the Iranian program by two to five years.

Of course, it will be necessary to factor in likely Iranian countermoves. The tried-and-true rule of combat is that "no plan survives first contact with the enemy." Since the adversary is not a cooperative collaborator in the planning process and has a very different set of goals and objectives, he will do everything in his power to derail his enemy's war plans. It is the responsibility of military planners to anticipate all possibilities, and to prepare plans accordingly. Since it is nearly impossible to anticipate all possibilities, the plans must be flexible enough to accommodate the unexpected.

As for whether such a military operation would be politically prudent or *strategically* effective, that is a debate that will undoubtedly continue until a plan is actually executed—or until the military option is decisively taken off the table.

Endnotes

1. Many writers and policy forums have recommended this approach. Three representative examples include: Thomas McInerney, "Target: Iran," *Weekly Standard* 011, iss. 30 (2006), Wisconsin Project on Nuclear Arms Control *Iran Watch Roundtables*, September 1, 2005, www.iranwatch.org, and Susan E. Rice, "We Need a Real Iran Policy," *Washington Post*, December 30, 2004, A27.

2. The view that military options should be completely discounted is in the minority. Two examples include: George Perkovich, "Now Is Time for U.S., Iran to Have Their Overdue Talk," *San Jose Mercury News*, November 2, 2003; "Dealing With Iran's Nuclear Program," International Crisis Group *Middle East Report* no. 18 (2003).

3. Col. Sam Gardiner, USAF (ret.), *The End of "Summer Diplomacy:" Assessing U.S. Military Options on Iran* (Washington: The Century Foundation, 2006), http://www.tcf.org/publications/internationalaffairs/gardiner_summer_diplomacy.pdf.

4. *Department of Defense Dictionary of Military and Associated Terms*, Joint Publication 1-02, April 12, 2001 (as amended through October 16, 2006).

5. A good discussion of initial and latter views on the tactical and strategic impact of Desert Fox is contained in Mark J. Conversino, "Operation Desert Fox: Effectiveness With Unintended Effects," *Air and Space Power Journal*, July 2005, http://www.airpower.maxwell.af.mil/airchronicles/cc/conversino.html.

6. This analysis was performed in preparation for a U.S. Central Command contingency planning wargame, as reported in a declassified briefing. See "Post Saddam Iraq: The Wargame," National Security Archive *Electronic Briefing Book* no. 207, November 4, 2006.

7. The sequencing of operations and numbers of forces presented here are notional, and not based on actual planning or any former or existing plan. They were developed by extrapolation from similar operations that are a matter of public record.

8. The numbers of aircraft are highly dependent on adequate basing arrangements granted by friendly nations within the striking range of each type of aircraft. Some long-range bombers may fly missions approaching 40 hours, while smaller attack aircraft may need to be based within a few hundred miles of their targets.

9. When discussing options for dealing with hardened facilities that are deeply underground, the debate often turns to the efficacy of tactical nuclear weapons. This debate is beyond the scope of this article. The reference to classified systems and technical means does not include the nuclear option. Indeed, the vast majority of planners greatly prefer conventional alternatives to tactical nuclear weapons, for a number of strategic and political reasons.

10. The Israeli military used similar tactics, with great success, against Hezbollah medium- and long-range missile launchers during their recent engagement in Lebanon.

CONTRIBUTORS

ILAN BERMAN is Vice President for Policy at the American Foreign Policy Council in Washington, DC. An expert on regional security in the Middle East, Central Asia and the Russian Federation, he has consulted for both the U.S. Department of Defense and the U.S. Central Intelligence Agency, and has testified before Congress numerous times on the subject of Iran and U.S. policy options. He is the author of *Tehran Rising: Iran's Challenge to the United States* (Rowman & Littlefield, 2005) and co-editor, with J. Michael Waller, of *Dismantling Tyranny: Transitioning Beyond Totalitarian Regimes* (Rowman & Littlefield, 2005).

DR. STEPHEN J. BLANK is Professor of Russian National Security Studies at the Strategic Studies Institute of the U.S. Army War College. Dr. Blank has been Professor of National Security Affairs at the Strategic Studies Institute since 1989. Between 1998-2001, he was Douglas MacArthur Professor of Research at the War College. He is the author of over 500 articles and monographs on Soviet/Russian, U.S., Asian, and European military and foreign policies. The views expressed herein do not reflect those of the United States Army, the Department of Defense or any other agency of the U.S. government.

SAM BROWNBACK has been a member of the United States Senate since 1995. A member of the Senate Appropriations Committee, he recently completed a two-year term as Chairman of the Commission for Security and Cooperation in Europe (the Helsinki Commission). He is a former White House Fellow, Kansas Secretary of Agriculture and U.S. Representative.

BIJAN R. KIAN contributed to this volume while a Senior Associate at the American Foreign Policy Council in Washington, DC. In that capacity, his areas of expertise included international finance, public diplomacy and Iranian politics. Mr. Kian resigned from all private activities in August 2006 for U.S. government service.

DR. ROBERT L. PFALTZGRAFF, JR. is President of the Institute for Foreign Policy Analysis and Shelby Cullom Davis Professor of International Security Studies at Tufts University's Fletcher School of Law and Diplomacy. He currently serves on the International Security Advisory

Board (ISAB) of the U.S. Department of State, and is a member of the ISAB's WMD Terrorism Task Force. Dr. Pfaltzgraff's work encompasses alliance relations, homeland security, crisis management, missile defense, the development and conduct of gaming exercises, counterproliferation issues, and strategic planning in the emerging security environment. He holds an M.A. in International Relations, a Ph.D. in Political Science, and an M.B.A. in International Business from the University of Pennsylvania.

THE HONORABLE THOMAS J. RIDGE served from January 2003 to February 2005 as the first Secretary of Homeland Security of the United States. In that capacity, he was one of the primary U.S. liaisons in the international fight against terror. Before the events of September 11th, Secretary Ridge was twice elected Governor of the State of Pennsylvania, and was the first enlisted Vietnam combat veteran elected to the U.S. House of Representatives. A preeminent statesman, Ridge currently brings his expertise to a variety of issues, including security, international relations, economic development and civil institution building, as head of the consulting group Ridge Global.

DR. JAMES S. ROBBINS is a Professor of International Relations at the National Defense University in Washington, DC. Dr. Robbins is also Senior Fellow in National Security Affairs at the American Foreign Policy Council. He holds a Ph.D. from the Fletcher School of Law and Diplomacy. Dr. Robbins is a widely-published author in the national security field, and serves as a Contributing Editor for *National Review Online*. He is the author of *Last in Their Class: Custer, Pickett and the Goats of West Point* (Encounter Books, 2006). The views expressed in his chapter do not necessarily reflect the views of the National Defense University or the U.S. Department of Defense.

ROBERT A. SCHADLER is Senior Fellow for Public Diplomacy at the American Foreign Policy Council in Washington, DC. He served in the U.S. Information Agency for over a decade, including as chief of staff to the Director of USIA and as director of the organization's International Visitors Program. Mr. Schadler was managing editor of *The Political Science Review* for ten years, and has taught political science at Rutgers University. He was educated at Georgetown University and the University of Pennsylvania.

REAR ADMIRAL JOHN F. SIGLER, USN (ret.), is currently the Acting Deputy Director of the National Defense University's Near East South Asia Center for Strategic Studies. A thirty-four year veteran of the U.S. Navy, he served in policy positions in every U.S. theater of operations and during his final tour was the Plans and Policy Officer (J5) for the United States Central Command (USCENTCOM). In that capacity, he was responsible to the Unified Commander-in-Chief for resource requirements identification and programming, congressional liaison, arms control and treaties, strategy formulation, joint doctrine development, political-military relations with 25 nations, and planning for contingencies ranging from humanitarian assistance to major theater war. The views expressed in his chapter do not necessarily reflect the views of the National Defense University or the U.S. Department of Defense.

JOHN C. WOBENSMITH is Vice President for Development and Senior Fellow in Intelligence Studies at the American Foreign Policy Council in Washington, DC. A graduate of the National War College, he has over 40 years of experience in the national security field, specializing in intelligence, emergency operations, communications and computer security, and technical, legislative, diplomatic and corporate liaison. He is a recipient of the National Intelligence Distinguished Service Medal, the Secretary of Defense Meritorious Civilian Service Award and the National Security Agency's Meritorious Civilian Service Award.